RECORD GROUP 24

Preliminary Inventory of the Records of the Bureau of Naval Personnel

Virgil E. Baugh

HERITAGE BOOKS
2011

HERITAGE BOOKS
AN IMPRINT OF HERITAGE BOOKS, INC.

Books, CDs, and more—Worldwide

For our listing of thousands of titles see our website
at
www.HeritageBooks.com

Published 2011 by
HERITAGE BOOKS, INC.
Publishing Division
100 Railroad Ave. #104
Westminster, Maryland 21157

Copyright © 1960 Virgil E. Baugh

All rights reserved. No part of this book may be reproduced or transmitted in any form or by any means, electronic or mechanical, including photocopying, recording or by any information storage and retrieval system without written permission from the author, except for the inclusion of brief quotations in a review.

International Standard Book Numbers
Paperbound: 978-0-7884-3640-6
Clothbound: 978-0-7884-8663-0

FOREWORD

To analyze and describe the permanently valuable records of the Federal Government preserved in the National Archives Building is one of the main tasks of the National Archives. Various kinds of finding aids are needed to facilitate the use of these records, and the first step in the records-description program is the compilation of preliminary inventories of the material in some 300 record groups to which the holdings of the National Archives are allocated.

These inventories are called "preliminary" because they are provisional in character. They are prepared as soon as possible after the records are received without waiting to screen out all disposable material or to perfect the arrangement of the records. They are compiled primarily for internal use, both as finding aids to help the staff render efficient reference service and as a means of establishing administrative control over the records.

Each preliminary inventory contains an introduction that briefly states the history and functions of the agency that accumulated the records. The records themselves are described series by series, that is, by units of records of the same form or that deal with the same subject or activity or that are arranged serially. Other significant information about the records may sometimes be given in appendixes.

When the record group has been studied sufficiently and the records have been placed in final order, the preliminary inventories will be revised and the word "preliminary" dropped from the title of the revision. Meanwhile, as occasion demands and time permits, special reports, indexes, calendars, and other finding aids to the record group will be prepared.

Several finding aids that give an overall picture of materials in the National Archives have been published. A comprehensive Guide to the Records in the National Archives (1948) and a brief guide, Your Government's Records in the National Archives (revised 1950), have been issued. Forty-four Reference Information Papers, which analyze records in the National Archives on such subjects as transportation, small business, and the Middle East, have so far been issued. Records of World War I have been described in the Handbook of Federal World War Agencies and Their Records, 1917-1921, and those of World War II in the two-volume guide, Federal Records of World War II (1950-51). Many bodies of records of high research value have been edited by the National Archives and reproduced on microfilm as a form of publication. Positive prints of some 10,000 rolls of this microfilm, many of which are described in the List of National Archives Microfilm Publications (1953), are now available for purchase.

CONTENTS

	Page
Introduction	1
Inventory	5
General records, 1798-1950	5
Correspondence, 1850-1945	5
Letters sent, 1850-1911	6
Letters sent to the President, Congressmen, and executive departments, 1877-1911	8
Letters sent to the Secretary of the Navy and to or relating to naval establishments, 1850-1911	11
Letters sent to and relating to officers, 1850-1911	16
Letters sent to commandants, 1862-1911	18
Letters sent to and relating to enlisted personnel and apprentices, 1864-1911	22
Letters sent relating to civilian naval personnel, 1903-9	24
Letters received, 1862-89	24
Letters received and copies of letters sent, interfiled, 1885-1945	28
Indexes and registers, 1862-1903	32
Logs of ships and stations, 1801-1946	36
Communication "logs" and other records, 1897-1922	40
Muster rolls, 1860-1956	41
Records relating to naval officers, 1798-1940	46
Application, examination, and appointment records, 1838-1940	47
Commissions and warrants, 1844-1936	52
Orders and related records, 1883-1903	53
Identification records and photographs, 1862-1939	54
Registers, rosters, and records showing complements, 1799-1909	55
Personnel jackets and other personnel records, 1900-1925	57
Records of service, 1798-1924	58
Other records relating to officers, 1863-92	60
Records relating to enlisted men, 1846-1943	61
Registers and lists of recruits, 1861-73	64
Enlistment returns, changes, and reports, 1846-1942	65
Continuous-service certificates, 1865-99	69
Records concerning discharges and desertions, 1882-1920	69
Records relating to naval apprentices, 1838-97	71
Other general records, 1861-1945	75
Applications and registers, 1861-1915	76
Records showing complements of ships and shore units, 1891-1913	77
Watch, quarter, and station bill books, 1887-1911	78
Photographic records	78
Cartographic records	79

	Page
Records of the Office of Detail, 1865-90	79
Records of the Bureau of Equipment and Recruiting, 1856-1928	83
Correspondence, 1862-92	84
Letters sent, 1862-89	84
Letters sent to commanders of squadrons and naval forces, 1865-83	86
Letters sent to commandants of navy yards and stations, 1862-85	88
Letters sent to other officers, 1862-85	91
Letters received, 1862-92	93
Indexes and registers, 1862-90	97
Reports of conduct and shipping articles, 1857-1910	98
Records concerning discharges and desertions, 1856-89	100
Continuous-service certificates and records relating to merit awards, 1863-1928	101
Records relating to naval apprentices, 1880-86	102
Other records, 1906	102
Records of divisions of the Bureau of Navigation, 1804-1946	103
Records of the Chaplains' Division, 1804-1946	103
Records of the Division of Naval Militia Affairs, 1891-1918	104
Records of the Division of Officers and Fleet, 1887-98	107
Records of the Naval Academy Division, 1851-1940	109
Records of the Morale Division, 1918-24	111
Records of the Training Division, 1917-40	113
Records of other organizations attached to the Bureau of Navigation, 1869-1913	116
Records of the Signal Office, 1869-86	116
Records of the Coast Signal Service, 1898	116
Records of the Board of Visitors of the Naval Academy, 1910-13	119
Records of units of the Bureau of Naval Personnel and of the Naval Research Personnel Board, 1940-46	120
Records of the Planning and Control Activity, n.d.	120
Records of the Office of the Chief of Naval Personnel, 1942-45	120
Records of the Special Services Division of the Welfare Activity, 1942-46	121
Records of the Recruiting and Induction Division, 1940-45	121
Records of the Naval Research Personnel Board, 1944-45	122
Appendix: Partial subject index to the general correspondence of the Bureau of Navigation	123

INTRODUCTION[1]

Naval personnel matters were handled by the Secretary of War from the establishment of the War Department on August 7, 1789, until the Navy Department was set up on April 30, 1798. From the latter date until 1815 the Office of the Secretary of the Navy was responsible for both civilian and naval personnel. From 1815 to 1842 the Secretary was assisted in personnel matters by the Board of Navy Commissioners. The burden of these duties led some Secretaries to recommend the establishment of a Bureau of Naval Personnel; no provision was made, however, for such a bureau, even at the time the bureau system was organized in 1842. One of the first important delegations of authority regarding personnel matters was made by Secretary of the Navy Gideon Welles in 1861 when he ordered Commodore Silas H. Stringham to take over the detailing of officers. When the Civil War came, Stringham was detached and an Office of Detail was created. This Office also handled the appointment and instruction of volunteer officers, the purchasing of ships, and related matters.

In 1861 Secretary Welles recommended the reorganization of the Navy Department and an act of Congress approved on July 5, 1862 (12 Stat. 510), authorized such action. The subsequent reorganization increased the number of bureaus from five to eight and established the Bureau of Equipment and Recruiting. One of this Bureau's chief functions was handling the enlistment of personnel. Its recruiting activities were carried on at naval rendezvous, as the recruiting stations were called, and on board receiving ships and other vessels of the Navy. The enlistment rendezvous were located principally at the large seaports on the Atlantic and Pacific coasts and, as there were no training stations, recruits were trained on board ship. The Bureau maintained both recruitment and service records, and in 1885 inaugurated the system of individual service records, or "jackets," still in use. An apprentice-training system was set up in 1875 (by authority of a law passed in 1837) under the Bureau's jurisdiction, where it remained until the Bureau of Navigation absorbed it some years later.

The Bureau of Navigation, also established in 1862, was assigned certain personnel functions, the most important of which related to officers. On April 28, 1865, the Office of Detail was placed under the Chief of the Navigation Bureau and for a time the Bureau was known as the Bureau of Navigation and Office of Detail. After being transferred

---

[1] Much of the administrative history for this introduction and for introductions to a number of sections of this inventory was taken from published and unpublished material prepared by Dr. Henry P. Beers, a member of the National Archives staff.

back and forth between the Secretary's Office and the Bureau of Navigation, the Office of Detail was finally absorbed by the Bureau in 1889. The Bureau of Navigation was at first mainly concerned with providing nautical charts and instruments, signal books, ships' libraries, and the like and with the supervision of the Nautical Almanac Office and of the United States Naval Observatory and Hydrographical Office. Another reorganization of the Navy Department was effected by Navy Department General Order No. 372 of June 25, 1889. By this order Secretary of the Navy Benjamin F. Tracy transferred enlistment and recruiting activities and the apprentice system to the Bureau of Navigation from the Bureau of Equipment and Recruiting. The latter Bureau was thereafter called the Bureau of Equipment and under it were placed the Naval Observatory, the Nautical Almanac Office, the Naval Inspector of Electric Lighting, the Compass Office, and, in 1898, the Hydrographic Office. In 1910 the Hydrographic Office and the Naval Observatory, which by this time had absorbed the Nautical Almanac Office (1894) and the Compass Office (1906), were returned to the Bureau of Navigation.

The Department was reorganized by Secretary of the Navy George von L. Meyer in 1909 on a divisional basis, and the Bureau of Navigation was assigned to the Division of Personnel. As prescribed by Changes in Navy Regulations No. 6, the duties of the Bureau of Navigation that pertained to personnel may be summarized as follows:

1. To issue, record, and enforce orders of the Secretary to individual officers of the Navy; train and educate line officers and enlisted men; supervise the Naval Academy and all technical schools; and enlist, assign to duty, and discharge all enlisted persons.
2. To establish the complements of all ships in commission.
3. To keep records of service of all officers and men, and prepare an annually published Navy register.
4. To handle all matters pertaining to applications for appointments and commissions in the Navy and applications from officers for duty or leave; report services performed by officers or men.
5. To perform certain duties with regard to naval discipline, rewards, and punishments.

When Josephus Daniels became Secretary of the Navy in 1913, the divisional organization established in 1909 was abolished and a new chief of the Bureau of Navigation was appointed. The Bureau retained its previous personnel functions and acquired additional ones. In 1908 the Bureau Chief had recommended that the Bureau's name be changed to Bureau of Personnel and the Fleet, but nothing was done about it.

An enormous expansion of naval personnel took place during the First World War, most of it through recruiting. Although recruiting ceased on August 8, 1918, on August 31 selective service was extended to the Navy and arrangements were made to obtain men through the draft. The Bureau continued its mobilization activities, trained enlisted personnel through its Training Division, and provided for the welfare, recreation, and entertainment of men in the naval service through its Morale (or Sixth) Division, which was established in 1919. In 1920 the Secretary of the Navy recommended that the Bureau's name be changed to Bureau of Personnel, but as before no action was taken. During the 1930's personnel activities increased still further as a result of the expansion of the Navy. From 455 vessels and an authorized enlisted personnel of 79,700 in 1933 the Navy increased to 907 vessels and nearly a quarter of a million enlisted men in 1941. Upon the outbreak of World War II in Europe, the building of the two-ocean Navy was accelerated. After Executive Order 9126, dated April 8, 1942, transferred the Hydrographic Office and the Naval Observatory to the Office of the Chief of Naval Operations, only personnel matters remained with the Bureau of Navigation. An act of Congress approved May 13, 1942 (56 Stat. 276), changed its name to the Bureau of Naval Personnel.

The administrative history of the Bureau of Naval Personnel and its predecessors is complex. Divisions came into existence as the need arose. Some of these existed only a short time; others had their functions transferred out of the Bureau; and others functioned without creating separate records, i.e., their records became a part of the general correspondence and other records of the Bureau itself. Only records created by divisions as separate groups of records are described in this inventory under the heading "Records of Divisions of the Bureau of Navigation, 1804-1946."

The records described in this inventory are the records of the Bureau of Naval Personnel and its predecessors that had been transferred to the National Archives by July 1, 1959. They are in Record Group 24, Records of the Bureau of Naval Personnel, and cover mainly the period from 1800 through 1950, although a few series date as early as 1798 and some muster rolls date as late as 1956. They amount to 15,485 cubic feet. Records of the Coast Signal Service are a part of Record Group 24 and as such are described in this inventory. The Service was in reality a Bureau of Navigation organization that was created to serve a special purpose and existed for only a short time.

Records of most Navy Department boards and commissions that dealt to some extent with matters coming under the cognizance of the Bureau and its predecessors have been allocated to other record groups and so have been omitted from this inventory. Records of some boards and commissions are with records of the bureaus with which their activities were mainly concerned; some are in Record Group 80, General Records of the Department of the Navy; and others are in Record Group 45, Naval Records Collection of the Office of Naval Records and Library. A <u>Preliminary Checklist of the General Records of the Department of the Navy, 1804-1944</u>, and a <u>Preliminary Checklist of the Naval Records Collection</u>

of the Office of Naval Records and Library, 1775-1910, both prepared by the National Archives, serve as finding aids to these records, the latter publication being cited throughout this inventory as Checklist of the Naval Records Collection. Other related records are in Record Group 37, Records of the Hydrographic Office, described in Preliminary Inventory No. 39, prepared by the National Archives; in Record Group 78, Records of the Naval Observatory; and in Record Group 181, Records of Naval Districts and Shore Establishments.

Chiefs of the Bureau of Naval Personnel and of the Predecessor Bureau of Navigation, 1862-1959

Name	Period of Service
Charles Henry Davis	Aug. 17, 1862-Apr. 27, 1865
Percival Drayton	Apr. 28, 1865-Aug. 4, 1865
David Dixon Porter	Aug. 8, 1865-Aug. 24, 1865
Thornton Alexander Jenkins	Aug. 24, 1865-Apr. 11, 1869
James Alden	Apr. 12, 1869-Sept. 30, 1871
Daniel Ammen	Oct. 1, 1871-June 4, 1878
William Danforth Whiting	June 11, 1878-Oct. 12, 1881
John Grimes Walker	Oct. 22, 1881-Oct. 21, 1889
Francis Monroe Ramsay	Nov. 1, 1889-Apr. 5, 1897
Arent Schuyler Crowninshield	Apr. 8, 1897-Apr. 28, 1902
Henry Clay Taylor	Apr. 29, 1902-July 26, 1904
George Albert Converse	Aug. 1, 1904-May 18, 1907
Willard Herbert Brownson	May 19, 1907-Dec. 24, 1907
John Elliott Pillsbury	Jan. 14, 1908-June 23, 1909
William Parker Potter	July 1, 1909-Dec. 2, 1909
Reginald Fairfax Nicholson	Dec. 2, 1909-Jan. 1, 1912
Philip Andrews	Jan. 1, 1912-Mar. 26, 1913
Victor Blue	Mar. 26, 1913-Aug. 10, 1916
Leigh Carlyle Palmer	Aug. 16, 1916-Nov. 1, 1918
Victor Blue	Dec. 19, 1918-July 21, 1919
Thomas Washington	Aug. 11, 1919-July 27, 1923
Andrew Theodore Long	July 27, 1923-June 7, 1924
William Rawle Shoemaker	June 7, 1924-Feb. 10, 1927
Richard Henry Leigh	Feb. 10, 1927-May 22, 1930
Frank Brooks Upham	May 22, 1930-June 30, 1933
William Daniel Leahy	July 1, 1933-June 30, 1935
Adolphus Andrews	June 30, 1935-June 11, 1938
James Otto Richardson	June 11, 1938-June 15, 1939
Chester William Nimitz	June 15, 1939-Dec. 19, 1941
Randall Jacobs	Dec. 19, 1941-Sept. 15, 1945
Louis E. Denfeld	Sept. 15, 1945-Feb. 21, 1947
Thomas Lamison Sprague	Feb. 21, 1947-Sept. 7, 1949
John Wesley Roper	Sept. 7, 1949-Mar. 30, 1951
Laurance T. DuBose	Mar. 30, 1951-Feb. 2, 1953
James L. Holloway, Jr.	Feb. 2, 1953-Jan. 31, 1958
H. P. Smith	Jan. 31, 1958-

RECORDS OF THE BUREAU OF NAVAL PERSONNEL

GENERAL RECORDS, 1798-1950

CORRESPONDENCE, 1850-1945

The Bureau of Navigation, after its establishment in 1862, followed the method of keeping correspondence that was in general use throughout the Navy Department. Incoming letters were bound in volumes chronologically by class of correspondent and outgoing letters were copied by longhand in volumes according to the same arrangement. Press copies of some of the handwritten letters sent were kept in other books. The correspondence was indexed in separate volumes.

In January 1885, pursuant to regulations issued by the Secretary of the Navy, this system was changed. The bound volumes of letters sent and letters received were replaced by a general correspondence file containing both types of letters. Thereafter the incoming letters were folded to a size 3-1/2 inches wide by 8 inches long, stamped, briefed, given a serial number, and filed in numerical order in wooden document containers. The identification stamp on the upper part of the first fold showed the name of the receiving bureau, the date of the letter, and the date of its receipt. This fold was also used for briefing data and, when necessary, for a stamp showing the number of enclosures. The serial number was entered in the "Briefing Record--Letters Received" (see entry 107) together with the date received, the file number, the name of the writer, the subject, and the action taken. Copies of letters sent in response to incoming mail were filed in press copy form on tissue paper in the folded file within the incoming letters and press copies of outgoing letters for which there were no related incoming letters were filed in envelopes. As a result of overlapping of the two systems, press copies of letters sent are frequently found in both the folded correspondence and the series of bound volumes. Besides the briefing record, the index to correspondence that was initiated in 1862 continued until it was replaced in 1903 by cards showing similar information (see entries 92 and 93).

The general correspondence for the period from January 1885 to July 1889 is missing from the Bureau's records in the National Archives. That it existed at one time is shown by the presence of the index volumes for that period and the briefing record that shows the file numbers assigned and the subjects of the letters received. The preceding volumes of bound correspondence were discontinued at the end of December 1884; the file numbers in the briefing record begin with 1 in 1885. The general correspondence in the custody of the National Archives begins in July 1889 with the number 3408, and the subject of this communication agrees with the entry for the same number in the briefing record. Except for the gap mentioned the general correspondence extends through the year 1945. The card indexes already referred to extend through 1943.

Although copies of letters sent were generally filed with related incoming correspondence beginning in 1885, some series of the former were continued in book form up to 1912. The earliest series of letters sent begins in 1850. Among them are fair, press, and typewritten copies, both bound and unbound. Beginning in 1912, in accordance with the general practice of most bureaus of the Department, the correspondence of the Bureau of Navigation was flat-filed by serial number in labeled and stapled folders. The system of filing correspondence by serial number was succeeded in 1925 by the subject-numeric system prescribed in the Navy Filing Manual. This system is still used by the Bureau of Naval Personnel and by the Navy Department as a whole.

Letters Sent, 1850-1911

LETTERS SENT. Jan. 2, 1885-Sept. 20, 1890. 20 vols. 4 ft.   **1**

Fair, typewritten, and press copies of letters sent by the Bureau to all classes of correspondents. Of the first two volumes, covering the same period, volume "A" is devoted to letters assigned odd numbers and volume "B" to those assigned even numbers. Letters for the remaining years are also numbered but the numbers do not follow the sequence of the letters. The subject is written above each letter in volumes A-I. The volumes are arranged alphabetically, A-T; the letters within each volume are arranged chronologically. For registers, see entry 103.

PRESS COPIES OF LETTERS SENT. Sept. 22, 1890-Apr. 28, 1896. 86 vols. 12 ft.   **2**

These volumes, of which all but the first five are numbered, contain press copies of letters sent. The volumes are labeled as to subject but their arrangement by volume number separates those with the same subject title. On the flyleaf of each volume is a cross-reference indicating the number of the preceding volume on the same subject. The subject titles (underscored) and a brief explanation (in parentheses) are as follows: Navy (to commandants of stations, training stations, training ships, cruising ships, receiving ships, rendezvous, officers, the Marine Corps, and the Naval Academy), Executive (to the Treasury and War Departments and the Pension Office), Certificates (to service personnel or their heirs relating to certificates of discharge, records of service, and pension claims), Department (Secretary's Office), Miscellaneous (congressional and miscellaneous), Appointments (appointments and revocations of appointments of petty officers), Complements and Transfers (of ships), Navy (except complements and transfers), Whereabouts, Prevent Reenlistments, Telegrams, Relative to General Orders &c., and Records. Many of these subjects are continued as separate press copy series for both earlier and later dates and are described in other entries. The volumes are arranged numerically; within each volume the arrangement is chronological. Most of the volumes are indexed alphabetically by initial letter of name, bureau, title, or subject. For registers, see entries 103, 104, and 108.

TYPEWRITTEN COPIES OF LETTERS SENT ("RECORDS COMMUNICATIONS SENT").
July 2, 1894-July 13, 1895. 26 vols. 7 ft. 3

These letters were sent by the Bureau to most classes of correspondents. Because of the fine paper and the elaborate binding, as well as the fact that typewritten copies were less generally used at this time than press copies, it is assumed that this is a special set, discontinued shortly after it was begun. Arranged chronologically. For registers, see entry 104.

PERSONAL LETTERS SENT BY THE CHIEF OF THE BUREAU ("PERSONAL LETTER BOOK").
Dec. 8, 1863-Sept. 5, 1874. 2 vols. 3 in. 4

Press copies of letters relating mainly to personal recommendations of applicants for positions, transfers, and other favors; confidential matters; and social affairs. Arranged chronologically. The first volume only is indexed alphabetically by initial letter of addressee's name, and thereunder chronologically. For registers, see entry 103.

LETTERS SENT CONCERNING THE NAVY'S EARLY USE OF AND EXPERIMENTATION WITH AIRCRAFT ("AVIATION"). Jan. 25, 1911-Jan. 8, 1912. 1 vol. 2 in.

5

Press copies of letters and endorsements sent by the Secretary, the Assistant Secretary, the Chief of the Bureau of Navigation, and a technical expert "in charge of Aviation" for the Department. Much of the correspondence is with "inventors" of airplanes, lighter-than-air craft, and a variety of devices for use in connection with all types of aircraft. The series also includes copies of reports to the Secretary on the progress of aviation in the Navy, answers to applications for aviation jobs, and a few letters to commercial airplane manufacturers who were seeking contracts to build planes for the Navy. Arranged chronologically. For numerical-record and subject cards that serve as a guide, see entries 92 and 93.

FAIR COPIES OF MISCELLANEOUS LETTERS SENT. July 24, 1862-Dec. 31, 1884.
9 vols. 2 ft. 6

These letters relate to business, administrative, and other matters not properly included in one of the special series of letters sent. Many of the letters are answers to inquiries from persons outside Government service. Apparently at least two volumes are missing from this series. Arranged chronologically. For registers, see entry 103. Press copies of some of these letters are described in entry 7; miscellaneous letters received for this period are described in entry 87.

PRESS COPIES OF MISCELLANEOUS LETTERS SENT ("LETTERS," "L" SERIES, ETC.).
Apr. 1, 1863-Dec. 31, 1884; July 3, 1889-Dec. 30, 1911. 258 vols.
27 ft. 7

These copies are duplicated, insofar as dates coincide, by the fair and typewritten copies described in entries 6 and 8. They are in numbered and unnumbered subseries, but all have the characteristic content of miscellaneous series. Arranged chronologically. Indexes in the volumes for the period 1863-84 are alphabetical by initial letter of addressee's name; in the other volumes they are, for the most part, alphabetical by initial letter of name, title, agency, company, or subject, and thereunder chronological. For registers, see entries 103, 104, and 117; for numerical-record and subject cards that serve as a guide to later records, see entries 92 and 93.

TYPEWRITTEN COPIES OF MISCELLANEOUS LETTERS SENT. Nov. 1, 1889-Aug. 20, 1891. 2 in. 8

These letters were sent by the Secretary of the Navy and the Chief of the Bureau mainly to private citizens. The copies are on legal-size pages, numbered 1-459, that apparently were intended for binding. Press copies of miscellaneous letters sent for the same period are described in entry 7. For registers, see entries 103 and 104.

Letters Sent to the President, Congressmen, and Executive Departments, 1877-1911

PRESS COPIES OF LETTERS SENT TO THE PRESIDENT AND TO CABINET OFFICERS ("EXECUTIVE BOOK" OR "A" SERIES). Jan. 15, 1890-Feb. 18, 1896. 5 vols. 9 in. 9

These volumes carry the subtitle "Cabinet Officers." Most of the letters were written by the Secretary of the Navy and the Acting Secretary, who, for a time, was also the Chief of the Bureau of Navigation. The letters relate to subjects of interest to both the Secretary's Office and the Bureau, including ship movements, personnel, intelligence, relations of the Navy with foreign governments and their representatives (especially insofar as naval attachés were involved), and other matters that came under the purview of the Bureau as a result of the 1889 reorganization. The letters are arranged chronologically. The volumes are indexed alphabetically mainly by department or title of Cabinet official. Some of these letters are duplicated by the typewritten copies described in entry 10. Earlier "Executive" series beginning in June 1798 are described in entries 4 and 10 of the Checklist of the Naval Records Collection. For registers, see entries 103, 104, and 108.

TYPEWRITTEN COPIES OF LETTERS SENT TO THE SECRETARIES OF THE STATE, WAR, AND TREASURY DEPARTMENTS ("A" SERIES). Nov. 2, 1889-Aug. 26, 1891. 1/2 in. 10

These letters were sent by the Secretary and Assistant Secretary of the Navy and by the Chief of the Bureau of Navigation, who was Acting Secretary for part of the period covered by this correspondence. These copies were probably made for the Bureau Chief because of this dual role and consist of loose sheets numbered 1-162, apparently intended for binding. They are probably duplicates, insofar as dates coincide, of the press copies described in entry 9. Arranged chronologically. For registers, see entry 103.

PRESS COPIES OF LETTERS SENT TO EXECUTIVE DEPARTMENTS AND MEMBERS OF
CONGRESS ("EXECUTIVE AND CONGRESSIONAL"). Feb. 10, 1896-Dec. 29,
1911. 413 vols. 42 ft. 11

These letters apparently continue part or all of the series described
in entries 2, 9, and 14. Arranged chronologically. Most of the volumes
contain indexes that have such headings as President, Houses of Congress,
Secretary of the Navy, and Navy offices and bureaus, under which entries
are by name and title of addressee. Earlier "Executive" series beginning in June 1798 are described in entries 4 and 10 of the <u>Checklist of
the Naval Records Collection</u>. Registers for letters before 1903 are
described in entry 108. The numerical-record and subject cards described
in entries 92 and 93 serve the same purpose for letters from 1903 on.

LETTERS NOTIFYING CONGRESSMEN OF VACANCIES AT THE NAVAL ACADEMY AND
AUTHORIZING CANDIDATES TO REPORT FOR EXAMINATION. 1877-79. 1 vol.
2 in. 12

These are fair copies of letters sent, followed by lists of Congressmen or of candidates to whom copies of the letters were sent. The letters are arranged chronologically; the lists of names, alphabetically.
The volume is indexed by initial letter of name of Congressman or candidate for examination. For registers, see entry 103. Press copies of
similar letters for a later period are described in entry 28.

TYPEWRITTEN COPIES OF LETTERS SENT TO CONGRESSMEN ("K" SERIES). Nov.
30, 1889-Jan. 30, 1892. 1/2 in. 13

These letters were sent to Congressmen by the Chief of the Bureau of
Navigation and the Secretary of the Navy. They are on legal-size pages
numbered 1-128 and were probably intended for binding. Arranged chronologically. For registers, see entries 103 and 104. For press copies of
most of these letters, see entry 14.

PRESS COPIES OF LETTERS SENT TO CONGRESSMEN ("K" SERIES, "CONGRESSIONAL").
Jan. 15, 1890-Feb. 21, 1896. 3 vols. 5 in. 14

These letters were addressed to Congressmen in reply to requests for
certain appointments, promotions, duty assignments, transfers, and detachments of officers; for the fleet or some vessel to proceed to a
particular place to participate in a celebration; to have Navy personnel
participate in such a celebration; for information concerning service
personnel and ships; and for vessels to be transferred or their assignments changed. The series also includes some copies of letters from
the Secretary of the Navy to the Naval Affairs Committee and the Committee on Appropriations asking for additional funds, transmitting bills,
and furnishing opinions on proposed legislation affecting the Navy Department. Arranged chronologically. The volumes are indexed alphabetically by initial letter of Congressman's name. For registers, see
entries 103 and 104. Typewritten copies of some of these letters are
described in entry 13.

FAIR COPIES OF LETTERS SENT TO THE COMMISSIONER OF PENSIONS. Jan. 1-
   Dec. 23, 1884. 1 vol. 3 in.
                                                                    15
   The volume contains copies of a special form on which data were supplied to the Commissioner of Pensions, who headed the Pension Office in
the Department of Interior. The data relate to naval service personnel
who submitted claims for injuries received in line of duty. Individual
jackets on officers and enlisted men were not kept until 1885 so that
most of the information needed had to be procured from logbooks and
muster rolls. Space was provided on the form for the date, name of vessel, name of claimant, information taken from logs, claim number, and
signature of the Chief of the Bureau. Arranged chronologically. For
registers, see entry 103. Press copies of most of these forms are described in entry 16. A series of letters received from the Pension Office is described in entry 74.

PRESS COPIES OF LETTERS SENT TO THE COMMISSIONER OF PENSIONS. Jan. 23-
   Dec. 23, 1884. 1 vol. 1 in.
                                                                    16
   These copies duplicate part of the fair copies described in entry
15. Arranged chronologically. For registers, see entry 103.

TYPEWRITTEN COPIES OF LETTERS SENT TO THE COMMISSIONER OF PENSIONS
   RELATING TO OFFICERS' SERVICE RECORDS ("M" SERIES). Feb. 4-Oct. 23,
   1890. 1/4 in.
                                                                    17
   These are copies of letters sent that enclosed or embodied service
records of officers. The copies are on legal-size pages, numbered 1-28,
that were apparently intended for binding. Arranged chronologically.
For registers, see entry 103. Press copies of these letters are described in entry 18.

PRESS COPIES OF LETTERS SENT TO THE COMMISSIONER OF PENSIONS RELATING
   TO OFFICERS' SERVICE RECORDS ("M" SERIES). Feb. 4, 1890-Feb. 13,
   1896. 4 vols. 7 in.
                                                                    18
   These are copies of letters sent that enclosed or embodied service
records of officers. They were apparently used by the Commissioner in
establishing the validity of pension claims. Arranged chronologically.
The volumes are indexed alphabetically by initial letter of name. For
registers, see entry 103. Fair copies of some of these letters are
described in entry 17.

LETTERS SENT TO THE FOURTH AUDITOR AND THE SECOND COMPTROLLER OF THE
   TREASURY ("I" SERIES). Jan. 15, 1890-Feb. 14, 1896. 5 vols. 8 in.
                                                                    19
   Press copies of letters, those to the Fourth Auditor relating to appointments, commissioning of officers, resignations, changes in duty
assignments, information from records, and other pay matters. The
Fourth Auditor headed the Treasury Department bureau that handled Navy
and Marine pay and other accounts of the Navy Department until October
1, 1894, when he became known as Auditor for the Navy Department. The
Navy Division of the Second Comptroller's Office was importantly con-

cerned in the settlement of claims made by officers and enlisted men and their relatives. The letters are arranged chronologically. The volumes are indexed alphabetically by initial letter of name of person, vessel, or, in a few cases, by subject. For registers, see entries 103 and 104.

LETTERS SENT TO THE SUPERINTENDENT OF THE PHILADELPHIA MINT. May 14, 1906-Mar. 27, 1909. 1 vol. 2 in.   20

Press copies of letters sent concerning the ordering, alteration, and return of medals and the accompanying additional service bars that were awarded to Navy men for service in the West Indian Campaign of the Spanish-American War. The manufacture of these medals was approved under acts of March 3, 1901, and February 27, 1906. The letters are arranged chronologically. The volume is indexed alphabetically by initial letter of name of ship served on, by subject, and by name of individual. For numerical-record and subject cards that serve as a guide, see entries 92 and 93. Copies of other letters sent concerning medals are described in entries 69 and 70.

Letters Sent to the Secretary of the Navy and to or Relating to Naval Establishments, 1850-1911

FAIR COPIES OF LETTERS SENT TO THE SECRETARY OF THE NAVY AND TO NAVY BUREAUS ("NAVY DEPARTMENT, A NO. 1" AND UNLABELED). July 26, 1862-Dec. 29, 1884. 2 vols. 3 in.   21

These copies document the relations of the Chief of the Bureau of Navigation with the Secretary's Office and with other bureaus of the Department. Arranged chronologically. Volume A No. 1 has a partial index. For registers, see entry 103. Press copies of letters duplicating most of these are described in entry 22. For a corresponding series of letters received, see entry 72.

PRESS COPIES OF LETTERS SENT TO THE SECRETARY OF THE NAVY AND TO NAVY BUREAUS AND OFFICES ("NAVY DEPARTMENT LETTERS" AND "C" SERIES). Mar. 30, 1863-Dec. 29, 1884; Jan. 15, 1890-Oct. 1, 1896. 9 vols. 1 ft.   22

The four volumes for the 1863-84 period contain copies of letters that are duplicated by the fair copies described in entry 21. The typewritten copies described in entry 23 duplicate some of the letters in the later volumes. The volumes in the series contain, in addition to letters sent to the Secretary and to Navy bureaus, some letters to the Hydrographic Office and to the Judge Advocate General. They document the highest level administrative relations of the Bureau of Navigation with these offices and bureaus and reflect the increased powers given the Bureau in the 1889 reorganization of the Navy Department. Arranged chronologically. Six of the nine volumes contain indexes arranged by office, bureau, or subject and thereunder chronologically. For registers, see entries 103 and 104. A corresponding series of letters received for part of this period is described in entry 72. Other letters to the Judge Advocate General are described in entry 25.

TYPEWRITTEN COPIES OF LETTERS SENT TO THE SECRETARY OF THE NAVY AND TO
NAVY BUREAUS ("C" SERIES). Nov. 1, 1889-July 1, 1891. 1/2 in.

23

Letters on legal-size pages numbered 1-127, apparently copied with a view to later binding. Arranged chronologically. For registers, see entries 103 and 104. For press copies of most of these letters, see entry 22.

LETTERS SENT RELATING TO THE GENERAL BOARD ("GENL BOARD"). Dec. 5, 1901-Mar. 25, 1904. 1 vol. 1 in.

24

Press copies of letters (some partially in code) and endorsements. Arranged chronologically. Indexed by initial letter of department, bureau, name, or by subject. Some of the endorsements may be registered in the volumes described in entry 115. For numerical-record and subject cards that serve as a guide, see entries 92 and 93.

LETTERS SENT TO THE JUDGE ADVOCATE GENERAL OF THE NAVY ("D" SERIES).
Mar. 6, 1895-Feb. 8, 1896. 2 vols. 4 in.

25

Press copies of letters relating to matters handled by the Judge Advocate General's Office, such as courts martial, courts of inquiry, boards of investigation, and boards for examination of officers; rank, precedence, promotions, and retirements; legislative matters and court proceedings; control of naval prisoners and prisoners of war; and reports on questions of international law. Most of the letters furnish or request information or refer to the Judge Advocate General matters that would normally come under his purview. Arranged chronologically. The volumes are indexed alphabetically by initial letter of name, vessel, yard, or subject; most entries appear under the general heading "Judge Advocate General." For registers, see entry 104. For other letters sent to the Judge Advocate General, see entry 22.

LETTERS SENT TO THE HYDROGRAPHIC OFFICE, NAVAL OBSERVATORY, NAVAL ACADEMY, AND NAUTICAL ALMANAC OFFICE. Jan. 22-Dec. 30, 1884. 1 vol. 1 in.

26

Press copies of letters concerning administrative activities in relation to these establishments, all of which were under the Bureau of Navigation at this time except the Naval Academy. Arranged chronologically. For registers, see entry 103. Fair copies of letters sent to all but one of these establishments are described in entries 27, 30, and 31; letters received from the Nautical Almanac Office and the Naval Observatory are described in entries 75, and 77.

LETTERS SENT TO AND RELATING TO THE NAVAL ACADEMY. July 17, 1850-Mar. 19, 1863; Mar. 29, 1883-Dec. 3, 1884. 2 vols. 5 in.

27

Fair copies of letters sent by the Bureau of Navigation and, in the earlier volume, by the Bureau of Ordnance and Hydrography. The Academy was under the jurisdiction of the latter from 1850 to July 5, 1862. The letters in both volumes are concerned mainly with high-level administrative matters. Arranged chronologically. The earlier volume is indexed alphabetically by name of correspondent, with separate sections for letters sent to the Secretary of the Navy and to the Superintendent of the Academy; the second volume is indexed chronologically. For registers, see entry 103. Press copies of letters sent for a later period are described in entry 29.

LETTERS SENT CONCERNING VACANCIES, EXAMINATIONS, AND APPOINTMENTS AT THE NAVAL ACADEMY. Mar. 8, 1886-July 5, 1889; May 14, 1895-Sept. 6, 1895; Apr. 2, 1903-Dec. 30, 1911. 130 vols. 14 ft.   28

Press copies of letters, including form letters, telegrams, and endorsements, that were sent mainly to Congressmen or to applicants for admission to the Academy. The letters relate to vacancies, applications, examinations, and appointments to the Academy, to the resignation and reinstatement of midshipmen and former midshipmen, and to appointments to the Board of Visitors or other positions at the Academy. Arranged chronologically. There are several separately numbered subseries, all arranged chronologically. The first five volumes are indexed alphabetically by initial letter of correspondent's or candidate's name; the others are indexed alphabetically by such general headings as "Congressmen" and thereunder alphabetically by name of person. For registers, see entries 103-105; for numerical-record and subject cards that serve as guides to the later records, see entries 92 and 93. Some of the letters described in entry 29 for the period July 1889-February 1896 are the same type as those in this series.

LETTERS SENT TO THE NAVAL ACADEMY ("N" SERIES). July 1, 1889-Feb. 8, 1896. 10 vols. 1 ft.   29

Press copies of letters sent after the reorganization of the Navy Department in 1889 that transferred the Academy from the Secretary's Office back to the Bureau of Navigation. Many of the letters in the earliest volume were signed by the Secretary. In addition to copies of regular administrative correspondence with the Academy, this series includes copies of letters sent to Congressmen informing them of vacancies at the Academy from their districts and permits to candidates to report for examination. Arranged chronologically. The volumes are indexed alphabetically by initial letter of name. For registers, see entries 103 and 104. Fair copies of earlier letters sent to the Academy are described in entry 27; press copies of some letters are described in entry 26.

LETTERS SENT TO THE NAVAL OBSERVATORY. Dec. 6, 1862-Dec. 30, 1884. 2 vols. 5 in.   30

Fair copies of letters addressed to the Superintendent of the Naval Observatory. The earlier volume is labeled as containing correspondence with the Depot of Charts and Instruments, a predecessor of the United States Naval Observatory and Hydrographical Office, the latter established in December 1854. On August 1, 1866, the Naval Observatory and the Hydrographic Office were made separate units. The letters relate to the procurement and supply of chronometers, compasses, and other instruments; the distribution of charts, copies of the <u>Nautical Almanac</u>, and certain technical books carried on board vessels; and housekeeping matters. Arranged chronologically. The earlier volume contains a chronological index for letters through April 22, 1863. For registers, see entry 103. Some press copies of letters to the Naval Observatory are described in entry 26.

LETTERS SENT TO THE NAUTICAL ALMANAC OFFICE. Aug. 4, 1862-Dec. 5, 1884. 1 vol. 2 in.   <u>31</u>

Fair copies of letters relating to administrative and financial relations between the Bureau of Navigation and the Office, especially the preparation and distribution of the <u>American Ephemeris and Nautical Almanac</u> and other publications. Arranged chronologically. For registers, see entry 103. Some press copies of letters sent are described in entry 26. A corresponding series of letters received is described in entry 75.

LETTERS SENT TO THE SIGNAL OFFICE. Jan. 11, 1871-Dec. 10, 1883. 1 vol. 2 in.   <u>32</u>

Fair copies of letters sent to the Signal Office, relating to technical experimental and signal matters as well as to administrative, housekeeping, and financial matters. The Signal Office, organized in 1869, was attached to the Bureau of Navigation. The letters are arranged chronologically. A note in this volume reads "For letters of 1884 see Letters to Navy Department.'" The series referred to is probably the one described in entry 21. For registers, see entry 103. A corresponding series of letters received is described in entry 78. Records of the Signal Office are described in entries 425 and 426.

ENDORSEMENTS REFERRING LETTERS RECEIVED BY THE BUREAU ("ENDORSEMENTS," "REFERENCES"). Nov. 22, 1872-Dec. 31, 1884. 3 vols. 3 in.   <u>33</u>
Press copies of endorsements by the Chief Clerk of the Bureau of Navigation, referring correspondence to administrative units of the Bureau. Arranged chronologically. For registers, see entry 103.

MEMORANDUMS, ENDORSEMENTS, AND LETTERS SENT. Aug. 14, 1866-June 13, 1884; Jan. 25, 1898-Jan. 3, 1901; Aug. 27-Oct. 21, 1902. 4 vols. 4 in.   <u>34</u>

This series, in three subseries as indicated by the dates above, consists of press copies of (1) mainly intrabureau memorandums, although a few are addressed to the Secretary of the Navy, from the Chief of the Bureau or the Chief Clerk, relating to technical matters such as navigation, administration, finance, regulations, standards, and procedures; personnel; supply; and miscellaneous routine matters; arranged chronologically; (2) memorandums sent to the Secretary of the Navy by the Chief of the Bureau, relating mainly to the transmission of service records of enlisted men, enlistment regulations, quotas, and complements; arranged chronologically and indexed in general alphabetically by name and subject; (3) unofficial memorandums, letters, and endorsements containing suggestions that were not yet in the form of official orders, regulations, or circulars, or information and instructions that were sent through unofficial channels. Arranged chronologically.

LETTERS SENT THAT CONCERN RECRUITING ("RECRUITING"). May 27, 1905-
Dec. 30, 1911. 53 vols. 6 ft. 35
Press copies of letters, including form letters, endorsements, and telegrams, that contain orders to recruiting ships, parties, and stations. The letters are concerned with the regulation of recruiting activities, including administration and financing of the program, publicity, transportation of recruits, assignments and transfers of apprentice seamen and officers detailed to recruiting duty, and waiving of certain requirements for enlistment. Arranged chronologically. The volumes are indexed alphabetically under such general headings as name of bureau or other Government agency, place where recruiting station was located, and name of ship and thereunder chronologically. For numerical-record and subject cards that serve as a guide, see entries 92 and 93.

ENDORSEMENTS REFERRING LETTERS TO THE BUREAU OF MEDICINE AND SURGERY
("M & S"). Mar. 7, 1906-Dec. 30, 1911. 10 vols. 1 ft. 36
Press copies of endorsements, most of which forwarded letters to the Bureau of Medicine and Surgery, containing recommendations or information. The letters, for the most part, requested examinations for ratings in the Hospital Corps, higher ratings, transfers, leave, and waiver of physical requirements for enlistment. The endorsements reported personnel actions already taken; asked for overdue reports; reported deaths, illnesses, and epidemics; and requested opinions as to the physical fitness of men seeking reenlistment or in whom physical defects were discovered after enlistment. Arranged chronologically. Indexed alphabetically by initial letter of name of correspondent, vessel, recruiting office, or station. For numerical-record and subject cards that serve as a guide, see entries 92 and 93.

LETTERS SENT CONCERNING HYDROGRAPHIC MATTERS ("HYDRO. OFFICE"). July 15,
1910-May 22, 1911. 1 vol. 1 in. 37
Press copies of letters, including endorsements, telegrams, and memorandums, sent by the Bureau of Navigation, with a few sent by the Secretary of the Navy. Many of the endorsements accompany correspondence being referred to the Hydrographic Office. The letters relate to the administration and policy of the Office; the furnishing of hydrographic information to Members of Congress; the procurement of men to serve on hydrographic expeditions; technical hydrographic instructions or information sent to the field hydrographic units and to fleets, squadrons, and officers commanding vessels; and appropriations to be used for hydrographic purposes. Arranged chronologically. Indexed alphabetically by

initial letter of department, bureau, fleet, yard, station, or ship, and, in a few cases, by name of individual. For numerical-record and subject cards that serve as a guide, see entries 92 and 93. Copies of earlier letters sent to the Hydrographic Office are described in entries 26 and 30.

Letters Sent to and Relating to Officers, 1850-1911

See also entries 15-18 for letters sent to the Commissioner of Pensions relating to officers.

LETTERS SENT TO OFFICERS OF THE ENGINEER CORPS. Dec. 3, 1850-Oct. 12, 1899. 10 vols. 3 ft.   38

Fair copies of letters sent by the Bureau of Ordnance and Hydrography and later by the Bureau of Navigation, together with some sent by the Secretary of the Navy. They are mainly orders transferring, detaching, or reassigning engineer officers. Arranged chronologically. Each volume is indexed alphabetically by name of officer. For registers, see entries 103-105.

LETTERS SENT TO NAVIGATION OFFICERS ("OFFICES OF NAVIGATION," "NAVIGATION OFFICERS"). July 28, 1862-Mar. 13, 1869. 5 vols. 1 ft.   39

Fair copies of letters addressed to navigation officers at navy yards, relating mainly to the furnishing of navigational instruments and technical and instructional literature. A few letters relate to projected navigational and hydrographic surveys. Arranged chronologically. For registers, see entry 103. Letters received from navigation officers are described in entry 80.

LETTERS SENT TO NAVY AGENTS, PAY OFFICERS, AND STOREKEEPERS. Aug. 2, 1862-Dec. 31, 1884. 5 vols. 1 ft.   40

Fair copies of letters sent, through June 18, 1868, mainly to Navy agents and storekeepers; after that date, to paymasters, pay directors, and pay inspectors at Navy yards and stations, at the Naval Academy, and on vessels. The letters relate to approvals of requisitions and vouchers for stores, supplies, salaries, and services; and to authorizations to expend money under pertinent Bureau and departmental appropriations. Arranged chronologically. For registers, see entry 103. Press copies of letters sent to paymasters during 1884 are described in entry 44. Letters received from paymasters during this period are described in entry 81.

PRESS COPIES OF LETTERS SENT TO OFFICERS. Dec. 17, 1862-Dec. 31, 1884. 101 vols. 11 ft.   41

These letters were sent, during most of the period, by the Bureau of Navigation and Office of Detail, which issued orders to and detailed both staff and line officers. The Office of Detail was not separated from the Bureau until October 1, 1884. The letters in this series are arranged chronologically. The first 15 volumes are indexed alphabetically by name of addressee, with entries thereunder arranged chronologically. For registers, see entry 103. Most of these letters are duplicated by the fair copies described in entry 42; press copies of letters for later dates are described in entries 46 and 50. A corresponding series of letters received from officers is described in entry 79.

FAIR COPIES OF LETTERS SENT TO OFFICERS. Mar. 2, 1863-Dec. 31, 1884. 6 vols. 1 ft. 42

These letters were addressed mainly to commanders of fleets, squadrons, flotillas, and vessels. The letters relate to the furnishing of navigational, hydrographic, and signal instruments and other apparatus; the supplying of charts and literature; experimental and scientific matters; navigational observations; orders and instructions; personnel; correction of circulars and manuals; and miscellaneous administrative and financial matters. Arranged chronologically. For registers, see entry 103. Press copies of these letters are described in entry 41.

LETTERS SENT CONCERNING APPOINTMENTS AS ACTING ENGINEERS ("ACTING APPOINTMENTS, ENGINEER CORPS, U. S. N."). Jan. 2, 1864-Apr. 19, 1870. 2 vols. 6 in. 43

Fair copies of letters sent by the Secretary of the Navy and the Chief of the Bureau appointing officers or detaching them for temporary service in the Corps of Engineers. The letters relate to transfers, leave, and other routine matters. Arranged chronologically. The volumes are indexed alphabetically by name of officer. For registers, see entry 103.

LETTERS SENT TO PAYMASTERS. Jan. 22-Dec. 31, 1884. 1 vol. 1 in. 44

Press copies, mainly of form letters, sent in connection with requisitions made on the Bureau by paymasters. Arranged chronologically. These letters are probably entered in the registers described in entry 103. Some of the fair copies described in entry 40 duplicate the letters in this series.

TYPEWRITTEN COPIES OF LETTERS SENT TO OFFICERS ("H" SERIES). Jan. 15-June 28, 1890. 1/2 in. 45

These letters were sent by the Chief of the Bureau of Navigation as Chief and also as Acting Secretary of the Navy. The copies are on loose sheets, numbered 1-78, that were apparently intended for binding. Arranged chronologically. For registers, see entry 103. Press copies of these letters are described in entry 46.

PRESS COPIES OF LETTERS SENT TO OFFICERS ("H" SERIES, "OFFICERS GENERAL CORRESPONDENCE"). Jan. 15, 1890-Feb. 15, 1896. 9 vols. 1 ft. 46

This series, according to a note in some volumes, excludes letters to commanders in chief, commanders of stations, and officers commanding vessels. Arranged chronologically; an alphabetic name index is in each volume. For registers, see entries 103 and 104. The fair copies described in entry 45 duplicate some of these letters. For earlier and later series of press copies of letters sent to officers, see entries 41 and 50, respectively.

TYPEWRITTEN COPIES OF ORDERS SENT TO OFFICERS. Nov. 1, 1889-Oct. 3, 1890. 1 in. 47

These orders were sent by the Secretary of the Navy and by the Chief of the Bureau of Navigation, who was also Acting Secretary for a time. The copies are on loose sheets, numbered 1-226, that were apparently intended for binding. Arranged chronologically. For registers, see entry 103. A series of press copies of orders sent to officers, most of which are for a later date, is described in entry 48.

PRESS COPIES OF ORDERS SENT TO OFFICERS ("G" SERIES, "ORDER BOOK-- OFFICERS"). Jan. 15, 1890-Feb. 1, 1896. 42 vols. 6 ft. 48

These are copies of regular and form letters that contain orders relating to changes of duty, leaves of absence, travel orders, courts martial, courts of inquiry, resignations, dismissals, examinations, commissions, and the like. The letters are arranged chronologically. Each volume contains an alphabetical name index. For registers, see entries 103 and 104. Typewritten copies of orders to officers, 1889-90, are described in entry 47.

LETTERS TRANSMITTING NOMINATIONS OF OFFICERS ("B" SERIES). Jan. 15, 1890-Feb. 15, 1896. 2 vols. 3 in. 49

Press copies of letters sent by the Secretary of the Navy and by the Chief of the Bureau in his capacity as Acting Secretary for this period. Most of the letters transmitted to the President for his signature nominations of officers to fill vacancies and officers' commissions. Arranged chronologically. The volumes are indexed alphabetically by name of nominee or officer. For registers, see entries 103 and 104.

PRESS COPIES OF LETTERS SENT TO OFFICERS ("OFFICERS," "OFF."). Feb. 10, 1896-Dec. 30, 1911. 332 vols. 36 ft. 50

Include form letters, orders, telegrams, and cablegrams. This series appears to continue the series described in entries 41 and 46 but is described separately because the letters are not duplicated by fair copies as are most of those in the other series. Arranged chronologically. The volumes are indexed, for the most part, alphabetically by initial letter of officer's name. For registers, see entries 105 and 109; for numerical-record and subject cards that serve as a guide to the later records, see entries 92 and 93. A separate series of orders is described in entry 48.

Letters Sent to Commandants, 1862-1911

See also various entries under the heading "Letters Sent to the Secretary of the Navy and to or Relating to Naval Establishments."

LETTERS SENT TO OFFICERS COMMANDING NAVY YARDS, STATIONS, AND SQUADRONS
("COMMANDANTS, BUREAU OF NAVIGATION"). Aug. 5, 1862-Dec. 31, 1884.
16 vols. 3 ft. 51

Fair copies of letters sent that reflect the wide powers of the Bureau of Navigation over officers during this period. The earliest volume is labeled "Commandants of Naval Stations E No. 1" and overlaps in dates the letters in the next volume. Most of the letters are directed to officers commanding navy yards. Arranged chronologically. For registers, see entry 103. Press copies of some of these letters, for 1884 only, are described in entry 53. Letters received from commandants of yards and stations for this period are described in entry 83.

CIRCULARS AND CIRCULAR LETTERS. Mar. 21, 1866-Oct. 13, 1874; June 8, 1875-Dec. 6, 1884; Feb. 15, 1890-July 26, 1892, and May 15, 1896. 4 vols. 5 in. 52

This series, composed of the three subseries indicated by the dates above, consists of press copies of: (1) circular letters sent by the Bureau to navigation officers, commandants of yards, and officers commanding squadrons, stations, rendezvous, and vessels, arranged chronologically; (2) confidential circulars, also sent to officers commanding vessels, squadrons, and yards, arranged chronologically; and (3) Bureau information circulars, Nos. 1-17 and 72 (dated May 15, 1896), arranged numerically.

LETTERS SENT TO COMMANDANTS OF NAVY YARDS ("COMMANDANTS"). Jan. 22-Dec. 31, 1884. 3 vols. 4 in. 53

Press copies of letters relating mainly to matters handled by navigation officers, such as furnishing to yards or vessels routine supplies, navigation stores, navigational equipment, and official and nonofficial publications; conducting surveys and inventories of materials; and returning to or repairing articles for the Bureau. Arranged chronologically. For registers, see entry 103. Fair copies of letters sent to commandants of yards, stations, and squadrons, 1862-84, are described in entry 51; letters sent for a later period are described in entry 56.

LETTERS SENT TO COMMANDANTS OF NAVY YARDS AND STATIONS AND TO THE MARINE CORPS ("E" SERIES). Nov. 4, 1889-Nov. 5, 1891. 1 in. 54

Typewritten copies of letters sent by the Chief of the Bureau of Navigation, the Secretary of the Navy, and the Acting Secretary, who, for part of the period, was the Bureau Chief. The copies are on legal-size sheets, numbered 1-243, that were apparently intended for binding. Arranged chronologically. For registers, see entries 103 and 104. A series of press copies duplicating a part of this series is described in entry 55.

LETTERS SENT TO COMMANDANTS OF NAVY YARDS AND STATIONS AND TO THE MARINE CORPS ("E" SERIES). Jan. 15, 1890-Feb. 10, 1896. 5 vols. 8 in. 55

Press copies of letters and telegrams sent, relating to movements of vessels in and out of yards, commissioning and decommissioning of vessels, personnel appointments and transfers, disciplinary actions, and training. After the Navy Department was reorganized in 1889 the Bureau of Navigation had broader powers than ever before and these letters thus relate to some functions new to the Bureau. Arranged chronologically. The volumes are indexed alphabetically by initial letter of yard, person, vessel, or subject. For registers, see entries 103 and 104. Typewritten copies duplicating part of these letters are described in entry 54. Press copies of earlier letters are described in entry 53; fair copies, in entry 51; and press copies of a continuing series, in entry 59.

TYPEWRITTEN COPIES OF LETTERS SENT TO OFFICERS COMMANDING SQUADRONS AND VESSELS ("F" SERIES). Jan. 15, 1890-May 6, 1892. 2 in. 56
These letters were sent by the Secretary of the Navy, the Assistant Secretary, and the Chief of the Bureau of Navigation both in his capacity as Chief and as Acting Secretary. The copies are on legal-size sheets, numbered 1-486, that were apparently intended for binding. Arranged chronologically. For registers, see entries 103 and 104. Press copies of letters sent that duplicate this series are described in entry 57.

PRESS COPIES OF LETTERS SENT TO OFFICERS COMMANDING SQUADRONS AND VESSELS ("F" SERIES). Jan. 15, 1890-Feb. 20, 1896. 9 vols. 1 ft. 57
These letters and telegrams were sent by the Chief of the Bureau and the Secretary of the Navy. Some are from the Chief in his capacity as Acting Secretary. Part of the letters are addressed to "Commander in Chief, U. S. Naval Force on _____ Station." Arranged chronologically. The volumes are indexed alphabetically by name of squadron or station, ship, place, and the like, with entries thereunder arranged chronologically. For registers, see entries 103 and 104. The fair copies described in entry 56 duplicate some of these letters. For a later series of letters sent to ships, see entry 60.

LETTERS AND ORDERS SENT TO OFFICER COMMANDING THE BERING SEA SQUADRON ("O" SERIES). Apr. 21-May 18, 1893. 1/4 in. 58
Typewritten copies of letters and orders, mainly from the Chief of the Bureau but some from the Secretary of the Navy and the Acting Secretary, to Nicoll Ludlow, commander of the United States Naval Forces in the Bering Sea. This squadron patrolled the territorial waters of Alaska as provided by a convention between the United States and Great Britain dated April 18, 1892, and a Presidential proclamation dated April 8, 1893, prohibiting sealing in these waters. The letters contain information on seals and sealing as well as patrol activities. Arranged chronologically.

LETTERS SENT TO STATIONS, SQUADRONS, AND SHORE ESTABLISHMENTS ("STATIONS"). Feb. 10, 1896-Dec. 30, 1911. 222 vols. 23 ft. 59
Press copies of letters, including form letters, endorsements, telegrams, and cablegrams. This series continues the one described in entry 55, but has a wider coverage. The subject matter varies, as may be seen

by referring to the registers and cards mentioned below. Arranged chronologically. The volumes are indexed alphabetically by initial letter of station, yard, shore establishment, and the like and thereunder by name of person. For registers, see entry 112; for numerical-record and subject cards that serve as a guide to these records, see entries 92 and 93.

LETTERS SENT TO SHIPS ("SHIPS"). Feb. 10, 1896-Dec. 30, 1911.
   264 vols. 28 ft.   60

Press copies of letters, including form letters, endorsements, telegrams, and cables, that were sent to apparently every class of vessel. This series continues, in part, the series described in entry 57. Arranged chronologically. The volumes are indexed alphabetically, mainly by name of ship, with entries thereunder made chronologically. For registers, see entry 113; for numerical-record and subject cards that serve as a guide, see entries 92 and 93.

"DEPARTMENTAL" LETTERS SENT TO COMMANDING OFFICERS AND TO THE STATE DEPARTMENT ("DEPT."). Sept. 9, 1896-Apr. 10, 1900. 1 vol. 2 in. 61
Press copies of letters, telegrams, and endorsements sent by the Secretary, Acting Secretary, and Assistant Secretary of the Navy, by the Chief of the Bureau of Navigation, and by the Office of Naval Intelligence. In general the letters document the receipt of intelligence reports from ships and squadrons; forward intelligence publications, photographs, diagrams, and other materials; and inform commanding officers at shore installations that foreign dignitaries have been granted permission to visit such installations. Arranged chronologically. The volumes are indexed alphabetically by ship, squadron, person, or department, with entries thereunder made chronologically.

LETTERS SENT RELATING TO THE NAVY'S RELATIONS WITH RUSSIA AND JAPAN
   ("RUSSIA AND JAPAN"). Mar. 11, 1904-June 3, 1905. 1 vol. 1 in.
                                                                                  62

Press copies of letters, endorsements, cablegrams, and telegrams sent mainly from the Office of the Secretary of the Navy to the President, to the Secretary of State, or to officers commanding the Asiatic Fleet, the Pacific Squadron, or the vessels thereof. Some endorsements referred letters to the General Board and the Office of Naval Intelligence. They contain information on the progress of the Russo-Japanese War and orders to commanding officers in conformity with General Order No. 154, which embodied the Executive order of the President urging "all officials of the Government, civil, military, and naval" to maintain United States neutrality. Arranged chronologically. The volume is indexed alphabetically by department, bureau, station, squadron, or vessel, with entries thereunder made chronologically.

LETTERS AND ORDERS SENT CONCERNING OPERATIONS OF VESSELS ("OPERATIONS SHIPS"). Jan. 3, 1909-June 30, 1910. 2 vols. 3 in. 63
Press copies of letters and orders sent by the Secretary, Assistant Secretary, and Acting Secretary of the Navy to officers commanding ves-

sels. During part of this period the Chief of the Bureau was Acting Secretary of the Navy, which accounts for the presence of these volumes among records of the Bureau. The letters and orders are arranged chronologically. The volumes are indexed alphabetically by initial letter of ship's name. For numerical-record and subject cards that serve as a guide to these records, see entries 92 and 93.

Letters Sent to and Relating to Enlisted Personnel and Apprentices, 1864-1911

PRESS COPIES OF LETTERS SENT CONCERNING NAVAL APPRENTICES. Dec. 19, 1864-July 31, 1869. 2 vols. 3 in.   64

Most of these copies are duplicated by the fair copies described in entry 65. Arranged chronologically. For registers, see entry 103. A corresponding series of letters received are described in entry 86.

FAIR COPIES OF LETTERS SENT CONCERNING NAVAL APPRENTICES. Dec. 22, 1864-Sept. 11, 1869. 1 vol. 2 in.   65

These letters were sent to commanders of "school" or "practice" ships on which naval apprentices were trained. They relate to the administration of and supplies for the apprentice ships, and to such matters as the recruiting, discipline, discharge, general welfare, and instruction of apprentices. Arranged chronologically. For registers, see entry 103. Press copies of letters concerning apprentices are described in entry 64. Letters received concerning apprentices are described in entry 86. Other records relating to apprentices are described in entries 241-253.

LETTERS SENT TO OR RELATING TO ENLISTED MEN. Dec. 22, 1890-Mar. 3, 1891; Sept. 24, 1903-Nov. 4, 1904. 44 vols. 5 ft.   66

Press copies of letters, including form letters and endorsements, most of which relate to personnel and administrative matters involving enlisted men. The earliest volume, labeled "U-1," contains letters sent to both official and nonofficial persons and form letters addressed to the Commissioner of Pensions for use in adjudicating pension matters. The form letters contain information or extracts from enlisted men's records and from log books. The letters in this series are arranged chronologically. All volumes except the earliest are indexed alphabetically by initial letter of enlisted man's name. For registers, see entry 104; for numerical-record and subject cards that serve as a guide to the later records, see entries 92 and 93. The registers described in entry 110 serve as a guide to the letters for the period January 1896-December 1902 that are missing from this series.

MISCELLANEOUS LETTERS SENT TO OR RELATING TO NAVY SERVICE PERSONNEL ("MISCEL. NAVY"). Feb. 10, 1896-Feb. 22, 1903. 18 vols. 2 ft.   67

Press copies of letters, including form letters and endorsements, sent to men either in or formerly in the Navy, mainly enlisted men and warrant officers seeking return to the service. The letters relate to waivers of certain reenlistment requirements, changes in the character of discharges, extensions of leave, admissions to the Naval Home at Philadelphia, and the like. The series includes copies of many routine form letters telling applicants for pensions that their applications had been forwarded to the Commissioner of Pensions; copies of letters of commendation for acts of heroism, such as rescues at sea; and copies of letters concerning medals. Arranged chronologically. The volumes are indexed alphabetically by initial letter of name. For registers, see entries 109 and 110; for numerical-record and subject cards that serve as a guide, see entries 92 and 93. For other series of records concerning medals, badges, and other awards, see entries 20, 69, and 70.

LETTERS SENT RELATING TO SERVICE RECORDS ("RECORDS OF SERVICE," "R OF S"). Feb. 11, 1896-Dec. 30, 1911. 113 vols. 12 ft. 68

Press copies of letters, forms, and endorsements conveying records of service "to legal heirs who submit proof that they are such; and to Government, State, and other recognized officials"; letters applying for issuance of certificates in lieu of lost discharges, requesting removal of charges of desertion, and informing official and nonofficial correspondents of the whereabouts of officers and enlisted men; and interbureau correspondence, mainly requesting medical records. The service records furnished were for the most part those of enlisted men for use in connection with applications for pensions or other Federal, State, and local benefits. Many of the letters were sent to the Commissioner of Pensions. Arranged chronologically. The volumes are indexed alphabetically by initial letter of name of person for whom records were furnished or to whom the correspondence relates. For registers, see entry 111; for numerical-record and subject cards that serve as a guide to the letters from 1903 on, see entries 92 and 93.

LETTERS SENT FORWARDING CERTIFICATES, APPOINTMENTS, AND BADGES ("C. S. C., G. C. B., B. P. O."). Feb. 13, 1896-Sept. 4, 1903. 15 vols. 2 ft. 69

These are press copies of form letters used to forward continuous-service certificates, appointments, and good conduct badges. The letters are addressed mainly to commanding officers of ships to which the men concerned were assigned. Arranged chronologically. The volumes are indexed alphabetically by initial letter of name of recipient of certificate or badge. For registers, see entries 105 and 110; for numerical-record and subject cards that serve as a guide to the 1903 letters, see entries 92 and 93. For press copies of other letters sent relating to medals and badges, see entries 20, 67, and 70.

LETTERS SENT RELATING TO NAVY MEDALS AND BADGES ("MEDALS AND BADGES"). Nov. 3, 1908-Dec. 27, 1911. 9 vols. 1 ft. 70

Press copies of letters relating mainly to awards made for participation in the Spanish, Philippine, China, and West Indian Campaigns and in the Civil War. Most of the series consists of form letters used for transmitting free medals and badges to recipients, either directly or through their commanding officers. Also included are letters requesting proof of identity or granting permission to purchase badges and medals from commercial firms, letters refusing awards, and letters to manufacturing firms that sought contracts to manufacture medals and badges. Arranged chronologically. The volumes are indexed alphabetically by initial letter of name of recipient or correspondent. For numerical-record and subject cards that serve as a guide, see entries 92 and 93. For press copies of other letters sent relating to medals and badges, see entries 20, 67, and 69; for other records relating to Navy awards, see entries, 85 and 370-372A.

Letters Sent Relating to Civilian Naval Personnel, 1903-9

LETTERS, REPORTS, AND MEMORANDUMS SENT CONCERNING CIVILIAN PERSONNEL. Feb. 2, 1903-July 30, 1909. 1 vol. 1 in. 71
This series of press copies includes transcripts of service records showing duties, dates of employment, rates of pay, and other personnel data; letters, reports, and memorandums relating to personnel changes; and letters or reports containing statements of functions and job descriptions. Arranged chronologically. For numerical-record and subject cards that serve as a guide, see entries 92 and 93.

Letters Received, 1862-89

LETTERS RECEIVED FROM THE SECRETARY OF THE NAVY AND FROM NAVY BUREAUS ("NAVY DEPARTMENT"). Aug. 2, 1862-Dec. 31, 1883. 8 vols. 1 ft.
72
Letters, including form letters and memorandums, received from the Secretary, the offices of the Solicitor and Naval Judge-Advocate General and the Judge Advocate General, the Office of Naval Intelligence, and from the following bureaus: Steam Engineering, Provisions and Clothing, Equipment and Recruiting, Construction and Repair, Yards and Docks, and Medicine and Surgery. Before 1865 the legal business of the Navy was handled by the Secretary. In 1865 the Solicitor and Naval Judge-Advocate General was appointed and served until 1870, when solicitors of all Government agencies were transferred to the Justice Department. In 1880 the appointment of a Judge Advocate General in the Navy Department was authorized. The series also includes a few letters from boards and from the Office of the Superintendent of Compasses, created as a part of the Bureau in 1873. Arranged chronologically. For registers, see entry 103. For fair copies of letters sent to the Secretary of the Navy and Navy bureaus for this period, see entry 21.

LETTERS RECEIVED FROM THE FOURTH AUDITOR OF THE TREASURY DEPARTMENT, THE NAVAL ACADEMY, AND THE NAVAL OBSERVATORY. Jan. 3, 1866-Dec. 31, 1868; Jan. 1870-Dec. 24, 1872. 4 vols. 4 in. 73
These letters are bound separately from other letters from the Academy

(described in entry 76) and from the Observatory (described in entry 77). The letters for 1869 have not been found. Arranged by establishment and thereunder chronologically. Indexed alphabetically by name of official from whom the correspondence was received. For registers, see entry 103.

LETTERS RECEIVED FROM THE PENSION OFFICE. Dec. 1, 1870-Dec. 31, 1879; June 1, 1882-Dec. 23, 1885. 7 vols. 1 ft. 74

Mainly form letters from the Commissioner of Pensions in the Interior Department, seeking information on service records of pension applicants. The verification of service and of injuries was, of course, important in the granting or denying of pensions and claims. Arranged chronologically. The first two volumes are indexed alphabetically by name of pension applicant. For registers, see entries 103 and 107. For copies of letters sent to the Commissioner of Pensions, see entries 15-18.

LETTERS RECEIVED FROM THE NAUTICAL ALMANAC OFFICE ("NAUTICAL ALMANAC"). Aug. 16, 1862-Dec. 13, 1884. 6 vols. 11 in. 75

Relate to administrative activities of the Office, the preparation and distribution of the American Ephemeris and Nautical Almanac, and technical matters arising out of the taking of astronomical observations and other scientific data, methods of compilation, and editorial questions. Arranged chronologically. For registers, see entry 103. For copies of letters sent to the Office, see entries 26 and 31.

LETTERS RECEIVED FROM THE NAVAL ACADEMY ("NAVAL ACADEMY"). Sept. 24, 1862-Dec. 12, 1883. 8 vols. 2 ft. 76

Relate mainly to administrative routine and financial management matters that were in the hands of the Bureau of Navigation. Arranged chronologically. For registers, see entry 103. For a separate series containing letters received from the Academy, see entry 73. For copies of letters sent to the Academy, see entries 26, 27, and 29.

LETTERS RECEIVED FROM THE NAVAL OBSERVATORY ("NAVAL OBSERVATORY"). Nov. 12, 1862-Dec. 29, 1884. 11 vols. 2 ft. 77

For the period December 1854-August 1866 the correct name of this establishment was the United States Naval Observatory and Hydrographical Office, although that name seldom appears in this correspondence. The letters in this series relate to the rating of chronometers and care of navigational and surveying instruments; the sending of time signals; the procurement and supply of instruments such as chronometers, compasses, barometers, and optical instruments; the distribution of charts and technical books; and routine administration and housekeeping. Arranged chronologically. For registers, see entry 103. For a separate series containing letters received from the Observatory, see entry 73. For copies of letters sent to the Observatory, see entries 26 and 30.

LETTERS RECEIVED FROM THE CHIEF SIGNAL OFFICER ("SIGNAL OFFICE"). Jan. 12, 1871-Dec. 14, 1883. 3 vols. 7 in. 78

Letters, memorandums, and reports relating to the administration of the Signal Office, the revision of the Signal Book, experimental and technical phases of signaling, instruction in signaling aboard ships, and laws and regulations affecting or authorizing activities of the Office. Part of volume 2 relates to early experimentation with the Very pistol, a device for night signaling with red and green lights. Arranged chronologically. For registers, see entry 103. Fair copies of letters sent to the Signal Office are described in entry 32.

LETTERS RECEIVED FROM OFFICERS ("NAVAL OFFICERS"). July 26, 1862-Dec. 29, 1884. 120 vols. 22 ft. 79

Letters and telegrams from officers commanding vessels, special units of fleets (such as naval forces on North Atlantic, European, and Asiatic stations), and naval stations, together with a few from the Light House Board and other establishments. Arranged chronologically. For registers, see entry 103. For fair and press copies of letters sent to offices during this period, see entries 41 and 42.

LETTERS RECEIVED FROM NAVIGATION OFFICERS ("NAVIGATION OFFICERS"). July 31, 1862-Dec. 30, 1884. 143 vols. 24 ft. 80

Letters and telegrams from navigation officers stationed at navy yards, relating mainly to navigational instruments; technical matters and navigational literature; and navigational apparatus, books, charts, binoculars, and navigation stores in general. The volumes also contain duplicate payrolls, invoices, and reports covering expenditures; some of the later volumes contain reports of navigation officers. Arranged chronologically. For registers, see entry 103. Fair copies of letters sent to navigation officers for part of this period are described in entry 39.

LETTERS RECEIVED FROM NAVY PAYMASTERS ("PAYMASTERS"). Aug. 1, 1862-Dec. 29, 1884. 53 vols. 9 ft. 81

Mainly transmittal letters for monthly returns showing money received and disbursed, abstracts of public bills with accompanying vouchers paid during a given quarter, statements of disbursements, and similar financial papers. The enclosures referred to are not bound with the transmittal letters. One volume, covering the period March 1-September 9, 1884, is missing. The letters are arranged chronologically. For registers, see entry 103. For fair and press copies of letters sent to paymasters, see entries 40 and 44.

LETTERS RECEIVED FROM OFFICERS COMMANDING VESSELS AND SQUADRONS. May 9-July 24, 1862. 1 vol. 2 in. 82

Most of these letters were received by the Bureau of Ordnance and Hydrography, since the Bureau of Navigation was not established until July 5, 1862. They relate chiefly to such matters as the furnishing of ordnance manuals, signal books, instruments, charts, and nautical almanacs. Arranged chronologically. Indexed alphabetically by name of officer and thereunder chronologically. For registers, see entry 103.

LETTERS RECEIVED FROM COMMANDANTS OF YARDS AND STATIONS ("COMMANDANTS").
Aug. 19, 1862-Dec. 30, 1884. 99 vols. 17 ft. 83
Include acknowledgments of letters received from the Bureau; letters transmitting requisitions, schedules, and payrolls for approval; and reports. Arranged chronologically. For registers, see entry 103. For fair and press copies of letters sent to commandants of yards and stations, see entries 51 and 53.

LETTERS RECEIVED RELATING TO SIGNALING AT SEA. 1869-89. 2 vols.
4 in. 84
One volume, labeled "1869-1884, Signalling, Miscellaneous Papers," contains letters and reports on signaling apparatus and tests such as those submitted by commanders of naval vessels. Except that the reports are grouped together, the contents of the volume appear to be unarranged. The other volume (1877-89), labeled "Signalling, Enclosures to Letters &c.," consists mainly of pamphlets, drawings, clippings, and manuscripts relating to systems of signaling at sea. Many of these bear the received stamp of the Bureau, an enclosure number, and the number of the related correspondence that they originally accompanied. Unarranged. For registers, see entries 103 and 107.

LETTERS RECEIVED RELATING TO MEDALS OF HONOR. Jan. 1, 1862-Dec. 31, 1866. 2 vols. 4 in. 85
Letters received from commanders of vessels and other officers on board ship and ashore and from the men to whom medals were awarded. The letters relate to the transmittal of the medals or acknowledge their receipt. Arranged chronologically. Indexed alphabetically by name of person. For registers, see entry 103. For later series of press copies of letters sent relating to medals and badges, see entries 20, 67, 69, and 70.

LETTERS RECEIVED CONCERNING NAVAL APPRENTICES. Dec. 17, 1864-Aug. 31, 1869. 18 vols. 3 ft. 86
Letters and reports concerning the training and progress of apprentices and related financial matters. Arranged chronologically. For registers, see entry 103. For copies of letters sent relating to apprentices, see entries 64 and 65.

MISCELLANEOUS LETTERS RECEIVED. July 1862-Dec. 1884. 62 vols. 11 ft. 87
These letters and telegrams follow the usual pattern of miscellaneous correspondence--from many sources and relating to numerous subjects. Volumes 16, 17, and 18 (May 30-December 12, 1867) are missing. Arranged chronologically. Volume 1 contains a partial name index, arranged alphabetically by initial letter of correspondent's name. For registers, see entry 103. For copies of miscellaneous letters sent, see entries 6-8.

Letters Received and Copies of Letters Sent
Interfiled, 1885-1945

GENERAL CORRESPONDENCE. 1889-1913. 2,337 ft. <u>88</u>
    Letters received and press copies of letters sent in reply, folded together according to the system for filing correspondence begun in 1885 (see p. 5). Arranged chronologically and thereunder by file number; a small quantity of correspondence dated as early as 1885 is unarranged. The registers described in entries 103-117 and the numerical-record and subject cards described in entries 92 and 93 serve as subject guides to this correspondence. The Partial Subject Index to the General Correspondence of the Bureau of Navigation, 1903-25, which is an appendix to this inventory, is helpful in using the cards. The index to officers' jackets, described in entry 192, may also be useful in connection with this correspondence.

GENERAL CORRESPONDENCE. 1913-25. 1092 ft. <u>89</u>
    This correspondence is a continuation of the correspondence described in entry 88, but the letters are flat-filed in folders. A few small groups of correspondence are filed separately, as follows: budget circulars, 1921-33; correspondence with publishers, 1913-14; tropical uniforms, n.d.; and transatlantic flights, ca. 1916-19. Oversize enclosures to this correspondence are described in entry 91. Arranged chronologically and thereunder by file number. For numerical-record and subject cards that serve as a guide, see entries 92 and 93. The subjects shown in the appendix to this inventory also serve as a guide to these letters.

GENERAL CORRESPONDENCE. 1925-45. 2,555 ft. <u>90</u>
    This correspondence, flat-filed and in folders, is a continuation of the correspondence described in entry 89, and shows the expansion of functions of the Bureau of Navigation (after 1942 the Bureau of Naval Personnel). Arranged numerically by subject and thereunder chronologically according to the system prescribed by the <u>Navy Filing Manual</u>, which was approved by the Secretary of the Navy in 1923. Legal-size and oversize documents that were enclosures to this correspondence are described in entry 91. The subject cards described in entry 93 and the card index described in entry 94 serve as guides to much of this correspondence.

OVERSIZE ENCLOSURES TO GENERAL CORRESPONDENCE. ca. 1916-45. 31 ft.
<u>91</u>
    These are oversize documents that were enclosures to the general correspondence described in entries 89 and 90. These documents were separated from the main correspondence solely on the basis of size and, except within small groups or fastened files, the 1916-41 records are unarranged; those for 1941-45 are arranged in accordance with the <u>Navy Filing Manual</u>. The lack of arrangement in the earlier records makes

any index or other aid all but useless except as the series of general correspondence (entries 89 and 90) may indicate the presence and nature of enclosures.

NUMERICAL-RECORD CARDS. 1903-25. 97 ft. 92

Each 3" x 8" card has a number that represents a subject of correspondence. On each card or group of cards representing a subject the correspondence is abstracted chronologically. The cards are arranged numerically, 500-58964; missing numbers represent the cards and corresponding officers' jackets that have been retained by the Bureau of Navigation. A select list of the subjects appearing on these cards is arranged as a subject index and attached to this inventory as an appendix. The cards can be used in conjunction with those described in entry 93 as subject guides to the general correspondence described in entries 88-90 as well as to series of press copies of letters sent, as indicated in the individual series descriptions.

SUBJECT CARDS. 1903-43. 52 ft. 93

These 3" x 8" cards were compiled in an attempt to list under more general subjects related correspondence in the general files of the Bureau. Many of the subjects appear on the numerical-record cards described in entry 92. The numerical-record card system was abandoned in 1925 and these subject cards apparently became the main "index." The subjects are those arising most often in connection with administration and answering letters; many subjects are identical in both series of cards. The cards in this series are arranged alphabetically by subject. In some instances there are numerical or other breakdowns under main subjects, as "Naval Districts," further broken down by number of district; and "Naval Air Stations," further broken down alphabetically by name of station. The cards in this series serve as guides to the general correspondence described in entries 88-91 as well as to series of press copies of letters sent, as indicated in the individual series descriptions.

NAVY FILING MANUAL CARD INDEX ("HISTORY CARDS"). 1925-42. 150 ft. 94

These 3" x 8" cards cover approximately the same period as the subject cards described in entry 93 except that they are classified and arranged according to Navy Filing Manual classification numbers. Each card usually contains the file number, a card number (in sequence for each file number), a subject, and a chronological listing of each piece of correspondence or other document. The cards can be used in conjunction with the card files described in entries 92 and 93; they index most of the general correspondence described in entries 90 and 91.

CIRCULARS, CIRCULAR LETTERS, GENERAL ORDERS, AND SQUADRON ORDERS.
ca. Apr.-Aug. 1905. 2 vols. 5 in. 95

These are typewritten and printed copies. One volume contains Departmental Orders, followed by Bureau Orders. The remainder of that volume and the other volume contain mainly orders to squadrons and individual vessels concerning transfers of personnel. The printed circulars, orders, and memorandums in the back of the second volume are from the commander in chief of and officers commanding units of the North Atlantic Fleet. Unarranged except as indicated.

CORRESPONDENCE RELATING TO UNITED STATES VESSELS ENGAGED IN THE MEXICAN
    WAR. ca. 1885. 1 vol. 1 in.   96

Includes typewritten notes, extracts from ships' logs, memorandums, and copies of letters sent by the Secretary's Office to the Commissioner of Pensions showing the periods of service of United States warships participating in the Mexican War from May 13, 1846, to July 4, 1848. Information contained in these notes and correspondence apparently resulted in the publication on April 6, 1885, by authority of the Navy Department, of a memorandum, a copy of which is pasted in the back of the volume. This memorandum shows the name of the vessel and the period of service as "Given by the Fourth Auditor" of the Treasury Department in one column, and as "Shown by the Log-Books and Files of the Navy Department, and Letter of the Bureau of Navigation to Commissioner of Pensions, March 9, 1885" in another column. In the front of the volume there is also a brief memorandum entitled "Navy co-operation in Florida War," the duration of which is given as "from Dec. 28, 1835 to A[u]gust 14, 1842." The records are arranged alphabetically by name of vessel. Records showing summaries of service of naval vessels in the Mexican War are described in entry 256.

GENERAL CORRESPONDENCE REGARDING NAVAL ACTIVITIES IN PANAMANIAN AND
    COLOMBIAN WATERS. Jan. 28, 1895-Nov. 19, 1904. 1 vol. 1 in.   97

Mainly letters and telegrams received and press copies of those sent by the Navy Department--particularly by the Secretary of the Navy and the Chief of the Bureau--relating to naval activities in and around Panama and Colombia during certain uprisings in those countries. The activities in which the Caribbean Squadron (North Atlantic Fleet) and the Pacific Squadron were importantly concerned related mainly to the protection of American citizens and their interests. The series also includes copies of orders issued by or to squadron commanders in chief and commanding officers of ships, and correspondence with the President, the State Department, the Secretary of War, and with the Office of Naval Intelligence and other Navy Department bureaus. Arranged chronologically. The volume is indexed by name of squadron, bureau, department, and the like. For numerical-record and subject cards that may serve as a guide for the records after 1902, see entries 92 and 93.

CORRESPONDENCE RELATING TO NAVAL PERSONNEL LOST IN THE SINKING OF THE
    MAINE. 1898-1901. 2 ft.   98

Includes letters of inquiry from relatives and friends of the deceased and press copies of replies; applications from relatives to the Advisory Committee of the Battleship Maine Relief Fund, with copies of replies; and records containing data relating to payments made by the trustee of this fund. The correspondence is arranged alphabetically by name of deceased.

CORRESPONDENCE RELATING TO THE AWARD OF SPANISH-AMERICAN WAR MEDALS.
   1905-7. 1/2 in.   99
   Consists chiefly of memorandums, many of which were prepared for the
Secretary of the Navy by the Chief of the Bureau, relating to claims
made by officers and men regarding their eligibility for medals. The
series also includes extracts from logs and muster rolls bearing on
these claims, a few press copies of letters sent to the claimants by
the Bureau, and letters received from the claimants. Unarranged, except where letters, enclosures, and replies are fastened together. The
numerical-record and subject cards described in entries 92 and 93 may
be helpful as a subject guide. Other records relating to Spanish-
American War medals are described in entries 20 and 70.

RECORDS RELATING TO THE TRANSFER OF THE CHIEF COMMAND OF THE PACIFIC
   FLEET. 1908-9. 1/4 in.   100
   Consist of a report of the Commander in Chief of the Pacific Fleet,
submitted to the Chief of the Bureau of Navigation, relating to the
operations of the fleet from July 1, 1908, to May 17, 1909, when Rear
Admiral Swinburne took over the command from Rear Admiral Sebree; an
accompanying folder of "Memoranda in connection with the transfer of
the chief command of the United States Pacific Fleet"; and a folder
containing a set of watch, quarter, and station bills for the U.S.S.
Yorktown.

CORRESPONDENCE REGARDING APPLICANTS FOR ENLISTMENT IN THE NAVY.
   1911-13. 3 ft.   101
   This series is in two parts, as follows: (1) letters, endorsements,
and telegrams received from, together with carbon copies of letters and
telegrams sent to, applicants and those interested in or sponsoring applicants as well as some applications for enlistment; and (2) letters
and telegrams received and copies of replies concerning such special
problems as reenlistment of dishonorably discharged men and waivers of
physical or other qualifications. Each part is arranged alphabetically
by name of applicant. For numerical-record and subject cards that serve
as a guide, see entries 92 and 93.

CORRESPONDENCE REGARDING DECEASED NAVY MEN AND MARINES. 1919-21.
   6 ft.   102
   This is correspondence of the Graves Registration Service at Paris,
and includes copies of cablegrams sent and received; correspondence
relating to the location, recovery, and shipment of bodies of deceased
Navy men and Marines and to the disposal of their effects; reports of
special boards relating to circumstances surrounding deaths and to other
matters; correspondence concerning group casualties and places of in-
terment; orders to enlisted men; and miscellaneous material relating to
such subjects as claims, personnel changes, and pay matters. Most of
the folders containing these records have both a classification symbol
and a subject, as "P. E. (Personnel, Enlisted)." Most of the records

relating to enlisted personnel are arranged alphabetically by name and thereunder chronologically.

Indexes and Registers, 1862-1903

REGISTERS OF LETTERS SENT AND RECEIVED ("INDEX TO CORRESPONDENCE").
July 1862-Dec. 1890. 28 vols. 6 ft. 103
Show entries for the general correspondence of the Bureau of Navigation, including the missing part (see p. 5) for the period January 1885-July 1889. Certain changes in the form and method of keeping these registers were made during the years covered by this series. From 1862 to 1884 letters received and letters sent were entered on the left- and right-hand pages, respectively. At first, names of persons and ships were entered in the same alphabetical series; by 1884 a separate alphabetical sequence was used for each such heading. In 1885 the use of separate volumes for letters sent and letters received was begun but was abandoned. Beginning in 1889 and continuing through 1890 entries for both types of letters were made on the same page under a single alphabet of names and subjects. The entries are arranged by year, thereunder alphabetically (as indicated above), and thereunder chronologically. A few volumes have special indexes in the front, arranged alphabetically by the first two letters, which are useful in locating entries under the main alphabetic headings, which are by initial letter only. References to these registers have been made in the descriptions of the individual series of letters sent (entries 1-71) and of letters received (entries 72-87), as well as other series.

REGISTERS OF LETTERS SENT AND RECEIVED ("ABSTRACT OF CORRESPONDENCE").
Jan. 1891-Feb. 1896. 14 vols. 3 ft. 104
Continue the series described in entry 103. The left-hand pages of the book are used to register letters received and the right-hand, letters sent, with references to the volume and page of the letterpress copybook in which a copy of each letter sent can be found. The volumes are arranged alphabetically; within volumes the arrangement is alphabetical by name of person, unit, vessel, town, or subject, and thereunder chronological. References to these registers have been made in the descriptions of the individual series of letters sent (entries 1-71) and in the series of general correspondence (entry 88).

SUBJECT REGISTERS OF LETTERS SENT AND RECEIVED ("CORRESPONDENCE / SUBJECTS"). 1896-1902. 8 vols. 3 ft. 105
One or more of these registers relate to each of the following subjects: Persons, Vessels, and Miscellaneous. All volumes for a given subject are not necessarily numbered consecutively. The main subject headings in each volume are marked by index tabs, which are usually alphabetical by name of person, vessel, or station, but are sometimes under such designations as "Naval History and Historical Subjects" and "Scientific Subjects." The printed forms and entries under "Received" and "Sent" are the same as those in other registers described in previous

entries, except that only volumes 1 and 2 have spaces provided under "Sent" for reference to series, volumes, and page numbers of letter-press copybooks. Under the subject headings in each volume the entries are made chronologically. Except in the first of the volumes, labeled "Persons," there are no separate alphabetical indexes. For partial index to the subjects in these registers, see entry 106. References to these registers have been made in entries 28, 38, 50, 69, and 88.

INDEX TO SUBJECT REGISTERS ("INDEX / SUBJECT KEYS"). n.d. 1 vol. 2 in. 106

This index, abandoned shortly after it was begun, was apparently intended to be a key to the registers described in entry 105. Entries in the index, made only under the letters "A," "B," and "C" under alphabetically arranged subject headings, refer to page numbers in volumes 1 through 5 of the subject registers described above.

REGISTERS OF LETTERS RECEIVED ("BRIEFING RECORD, LETTERS RECEIVED"). Jan. 2, 1885-Dec. 31, 1890. 7 vols. 2 ft. 107

These volumes are of more than ordinary importance because most of the correspondence to which they are a key is missing, as explained on p. 5. For the period July 1889-December 1890 there are only about 4 inches of letters received (a part of the series described in entry 88), beginning with file number 3408. The Briefing Record covers the following file numbers:

Year	Inclusive Numbers
1885	1-4376
1886	1-3830
1887	1-3943
1888	1-3737
1889	1-9346
1890	1-11917

It contains the following information for each letter received: date received, file number, name of correspondent (person, vessel, or administrative unit), subject of letter, and action taken. Symbols and letters were used to indicate the character of the action and a key to these is at the top of the page. Both the volumes and the entries within them are arranged chronologically. Parallel registers maintained during this period are described in entry 103. References to these registers have been made in entries 74, 84, and 88.

REGISTERS OF CORRESPONDENCE WITH EXECUTIVE DEPARTMENTS AND WITH CONGRESS. Jan. 1896-Dec. 1902. 7 vols. 2 ft. 108

The general headings under which letters were entered in the registers are: Government departments and subdivisions; bureaus of the Navy Department; boards and commissions; miscellaneous Government offices;

Congress; and Congressmen. As in other registers entries are made under the subheadings "Received" and "Sent," and give briefs of letters together with the volume and page references to series of press copybooks. The volumes are arranged chronologically; the entries are chronological under each heading except for those under "Congressmen," which are alphabetical. Series of "Executive" or "Executive and Congressional" correspondence are described in entries 2, 9, 11, and 88.

REGISTERS OF CORRESPONDENCE WITH OR RELATING TO OFFICERS ("CORRESPONDENCE OFFICERS"). 1896-1902. 8 vols. 2 ft.   109

As in other registers, the left- and right-hand pages have entries for letters received and sent, respectively. Entries are made under the officer's name, which appears at the top of the page. Each volume covers a section of the alphabet for given dates and contains an index, either alphabetical by initial letter of name or partly alphabetical. This index is necessary since the system of entering the names of officers is not apparent. The volumes are arranged chronologically, thereunder by section of the alphabet. Reference has been made to these registers in entries 50, 67, and 88.

REGISTERS OF CORRESPONDENCE WITH OR CONCERNING ENLISTED MEN. Jan. 1896-Dec. 1902. 6 vols. 2 ft.   110

These registers, each volume of which covers all or half an alphabetical sequence, have a straight alphabetical arrangement of names of enlisted men; entries for letters received and sent are on different halves of the same page. These registers are a key to part of the letters sent that are missing from the series described in entry 66 and to correspondence described in entries 67, 69, and 88.

REGISTERS OF CORRESPONDENCE REGARDING RECORDS OF ENLISTED MEN. Jan. 1896-July 1902. 2 vols. 6 in.   111

These registers contain the usual entries for letters received and sent, including briefs of the subject matter and references to the series, volumes, and page numbers of the press copybooks. The volumes are arranged chronologically; the arrangement within each volume is alphabetical by initial letter of enlisted man's name. These registers serve as a guide to letters sent that are described in entry 68 and to some of the general correspondence described in entry 88.

REGISTERS OF CORRESPONDENCE WITH NAVAL STATIONS ("CORRESPONDENCE / STATIONS"). 1896-1902. 4 vols. 1 ft.   112

These volumes register all correspondence with or concerning a given station, with entries for letters received and letters sent on different halves of the same page. Names of stations are not in alphabetical order and some subjects, such as "Hospitals," are used. Under the station name the entries are made chronologically. The main series of letterpress copybooks referred to is described in entry 59.

REGISTERS OF SHIPS' CORRESPONDENCE ("CORRESPONDENCE / SHIPS"). 1896-
1902. 5 vols. 1 ft. <u>113</u>

These volumes register ships' correspondence in sections arranged alphabetically by name of ship and in a separate section for smaller ships, with entries for letters received and letters sent on different halves of the same page. The section for smaller vessels has such headings as Coast Survey Ships, Fish Commission Ships, and State School Ships. The volumes are arranged chronologically, thereunder by name of section, and thereunder chronologically by date of letter. A "List of Vessels of the United States Navy" is in the front of both registers labeled "Vol. 4." The press copies referred to in the entries are described in entry 60.

REGISTER OF REPORTS AND LETTERS RECEIVED FROM NAVAL PERSONNEL ("REPORTS
AND LETTERS RECEIVED . . . PERSONNEL OFFICERS"). July 1891-Aug.
1895. 1 vol. 3 in. <u>114</u>

The correspondence and reports registered in this volume are those received by personnel officers of the Bureau of Navigation from commissioned and noncommissioned naval officers and specialists in the field. Most of the reports are fitness reports. Each entry gives the name of the correspondent, his rank, the file number assigned the letter, the date of the letter and date of its receipt, the name of the superior officer, the subject of the letter, and remarks. The entries are alphabetical by initial letter of correspondent's name and thereunder chronological by date of letter. The series to which the file numbers refer has not been located.

REGISTERS OF LETTERS RECEIVED AND FORWARDED. Aug. 24, 1895-Dec. 31,
1903. 2 vols. 4 in. <u>115</u>

Each volume has two parts. In the first part are separate sections for letters received from the Secretary of the Navy or from Navy bureaus, with entries in each section arranged chronologically by date the letter was received and forwarded. In the second part entries are arranged alphabetically by initial letter of correspondent's name and thereunder chronologically by date letter was received and forwarded. The letters to which the registers refer have not been located.

INDEX TO RECRUITING CORRESPONDENCE RECEIVED FROM THE BUREAU OF EQUIPMENT
AND RECRUITING. 1885-86. 1 vol. 2 in. <u>116</u>

The entries contain the following information for each letter: date, file number, name of writer, and brief of subject. Arranged within the volume by year and thereunder by number of letter. Indexed alphabetically by subject. The numbered correspondence referred to has not been located.

REGISTERS OF MISCELLANEOUS CORRESPONDENCE. Jan. 1896-Dec. 1902.
7 vols. 1 ft. <u>117</u>

These volumes register correspondence under names of associations,

35

business firms, cities, colleges, Naval Militia, periodicals, railroads, and the like. Under these headings the names of persons writing or written about are entered alphabetically by initial letter of name and thereunder chronologically by date letter was received. The volumes are arranged by chronological period. The registers contain references to other letters, most of which are the press copies of letters sent described in entry 7.

LOGS OF SHIPS AND STATIONS, 1801-1946

The task of collecting and preserving logs of naval vessels was performed in a rather haphazard fashion by various offices of the Department until the establishment of the Bureau of Navigation, which took over the task and assumed custody of such records. The earliest log in the collections in this record group is that of the U.S.S. Essex, which begins May 21, 1801. Many of the earliest volumes are in reality journals--that is, personal diaries of officers and enlisted men aboard U. S. ships that tell not only about the official activities of officers and crews but also about the private adventures, opinions, and reflections of the writers. They were maintained on shore or on two or more vessels and therefore did not originate as official records of one ship. Before 1860 there was little regularity in methods of keeping logs and the volumes in which the entries were made were apparently purchased by captains from stationers, either ready-made or made to order. Printed log forms appeared as early as the log of the U.S.S. Congress, 1816, but they were rare before 1860. Many captains retained the logs as their private property, since they were not held strictly accountable by the Navy Department. In 1860, however, the Department began to furnish printed blank books, of uniform size and character, in which all log entries had to be made. The form was changed slightly in 1866 and again at the end of 1915. Regulations governing the nature of the entries were issued and revised from time to time. Apparently in 1916 all the logs then on hand were labeled with the numbers of the cases in which they were shelved and were numbered within each case, beginning with the number 1. Until the end of 1923 the logs continued to be so numbered, but beginning in 1924 they were bound in post binders, labeled "L. L. L." (looseleaf log) and left unnumbered.

The terms "deck log" and "rough log" are synonymous and refer to the penciled log kept originally on board ship. The first "smooth" or typewritten logs were made in the early 1900's on forms in use at that time. At present the smooth log is copied from the rough log on the looseleaf forms prescribed, by typewriter if one is available, or in ink. Both the penciled copy and the certified typewritten or ink copy are prepared on board ship. The rough log is at present kept on the ship for 3 years, after which, with a few exceptions, it is destroyed. The smooth log must be submitted monthly to the Bureau of Naval Personnel and is considered the official copy. It is not always possible to send in the smooth copy, especially under wartime conditions, and in such cases the rough log is accepted.

Naval ship logs are now highly standardized as to both form and content so that there is little room for the personal accounts or observations that are found in the older logs. Usually the log consists of the following: a title page, a list of officers, a columnar sheet, and a remarks sheet. The title page, which precedes all entries for a given month, contains the name or identification symbol and the number of the vessel; the name of the commander; the division, squadron, flotilla, or fleet to which the ship is attached; and the beginning and ending dates of that particular log. The list of officers gives the name, rank, date of reporting on board, primary duties, and information on next-of-kin for each officer assigned to the vessel. The columnar sheet contains spaces for the name or identification symbol and the number of the vessel, the date covered by the log, detailed meteorological and hydrographic data, and instrument readings indicating the position of the ship; there are also spaces for recording general drills and exercises, ocean temperature and other information about the surface of the ocean, and "hydrographic and meteorological remarks." The remarks sheet contains whatever narrative account or information is considered important; it describes actions engaged in and lists those wounded or killed in action. In addition, logs often contain lists of enlisted men and notes on the condition and movements of the ship, the quantity of stores, and disciplinary actions taken. The health of officers and crews is recorded in medical journals that are forwarded to the Bureau of Medicine and Surgery. Engineering logs are forwarded to the Bureau of Ships.

The log is one of the basic historical records of the operation of naval vessels and of shore units keeping that type of record. The logs also have long-term administrative value as basic sources of information on the service of officers and men in the Navy. Such matters as claims, pensions, and other benefits are often proved or disproved by reference to accounts contained in these logs. The value of the logs for any purpose depends to some extent on the events in which the personnel of the ship or shore unit participated and on the amount and kind of detail recorded.

LOGS OF UNITED STATES NAVAL SHIPS AND STATIONS. 1801-1946. 72,500 vols. 8,060 ft. 118

Except for a few small separate groups of logs, these logs are physically arranged in three groups, each of which is a unit in itself, and cover three periods as follows: 1801-1914, 1915-40, and 1941-46. There is some overlapping in dates from group to group. For purposes of description the logs within the chronological periods may be conveniently classified as follows:

1. Logs of "name" vessels, i.e., most of the large Navy craft in use since shortly after the creation of the Navy Department in 1798 and

identified usually by name of vessel, as U.S.S. Arizona. With the exception of landing craft or other small craft used during World War II, all Navy vessels built in recent years have as standard nomenclature both a name and a symbol followed by an identification number, as U.S.S. Missouri-B-63. Most of the larger vessels are better known by their names; their logs are with those of the earlier "name" vessels and are arranged alphabetically by name of vessel, thereunder chronologically. This group also includes logs of vessels named on the basis of the group to which they belong; these logs are arranged alphabetically by name of group to which the vessel belongs, thereunder in numerical order (Eagle Boat #1; Eagle Boat #2) or alphabetically by place name (Receiving Ship, Cavite, P. I.; Receiving Ship, Charleston, S. C.), and thereunder chronologically. Among the logs of "name" vessels the following are of especial interest:

Name of ship	Type	Dates
Constitution	Frigate	Aug. 16, 1803-June 8, 1934
Constellation	Frigate	Mar. 15, 1802-Apr. 30, 1921
Kearsarge	Sloop-of-war	Jan. 24, 1862-Feb. 1, 1894
Maine	Battleship	Sept. 17, 1895-Sept. 30, 1897
Michigan	Battleship	Jan. 4, 1910-Dec. 31, 1921
Alabama	Battleship	Aug. 16, 1942-June 30, 1945
Enterprise	Aircraft Carrier	May 12, 1938-Nov. 30, 1945

2. Logs of special craft, usually smaller in size than the "name" vessels and usually identified by a symbol for the type of craft followed by the number of the individual boat, as S-51 (submarine), LST-790 (landing ship tank), and SC-1340 (submarine chaser). The logs for these vessels are arranged alphabetically by symbol of vessel, thereunder by number of vessel, and thereunder chronologically.

3. Logs of shore units located both inside and outside the continental limits of the United States, including naval stations, naval air stations, receiving stations, training schools, training units at colleges, section and operating bases, Marine flying fields, and others. A few logs of receiving ships are also included. These are unarranged, with the exception of a few groups arranged in part alphabetically by name of station or other unit and thereunder chronologically.

Indexes to the logs are described in entries 119 and 120. A detailed list of the logs has been compiled by the National Archives and is, with certain limitations, available to searchers. A series of logs, journals, and diaries of officers of the United States Navy at sea, March 1776-June 1908, 210 volumes, is described in entry 392 of the Checklist of the Naval Records Collection.

CARD INDEX TO SHIPS' LOGS. 1801-1940. 4 ft.   119
    Gives the following information: name and type of vessel; changes of

its name; tonnage; armament; date of building or purchase; list of volumes of logs (an entry for each volume, with inclusive dates); and date when vessel was decommissioned or sold. Some vessels are listed with the notation "No log received." The index is accompanied by a carbon copy of a list of logs from the earliest ones received to January 10, 1898. The cards are arranged alphabetically by name of ship; there is a separate alphabetic section for subchasers, arranged by number of vessel.

INDEX TO SHIPS' LOGS. 1801-1906. 1 vol. 3 in.   120
This is a list that was apparently kept as a tally record of logs received by the Bureau. Entries were made under the name of the vessel. The only arrangement seems to be by date of the first log received for each vessel. Indexed alphabetically by name of vessel. The information in this volume was transferred to the card index described in entry 119.

"LIST OF LOG BOOKS OF U. S. VESSELS, 1861-1865, ON FILE IN THE NAVY DEPARTMENT." 1891. 2 vols. Less than 1 in.   121
These are copies (one incomplete) of a small book printed by the Government Printing Office that listed logs for the period indicated. The name of the vessel, inclusive dates of the log, and the log number are given. "Chronological Tables" covering the same years show the principal engagements and movements of naval vessels.

LIST OF SHIP LOGS ARRANGED ACCORDING TO WAR PERIODS. n.d. Negligible.
   122
This typewritten list was apparently compiled in the Bureau of Navigation. The logs are arranged according to the following periods: Revolutionary War, 1776-83; Quasi-War with France, 1798-1801; Barbary War, 1798-1805, 1815; War of 1812, 1812-15; Mexican War, 1846-48; and Civil War, 1861-62. Arranged by period, thereunder alphabetically by name of log (except for the Mexican War period, under which the logs are unarranged).

"CATALOG OF LOG BOOKS IN THE NAVY COMMISSIONERS' OFFICE 13 JULY 1827 AND RECEIVED THEREAFTER TILL JANUARY 1863." 1 vol. 1/2 in.   123
Contains the log number, name of vessel, and inclusive dates. The earliest log listed is the 1803 log of the Constitution, the latest an 1863 log of the store ship Warren. Part of the entries are arranged by log number, part chronologically.

MICROFILM COPY OF LOG OF THE CONSTITUTION. Dec. 31, 1813-May 16, 1815. 1 roll. 2 in.   124
This negative microfilm was made as a security copy of the volume of the Constitution's log that was carried on the Freedom Train.

LOGS OF THE GERMAN MERCHANT VESSELS PRINZ WALDEMAR AND PRINZ SIGISMUND. July 1903-Aug. 1914. 52 vols. 3 ft.   125
Logs of the Prinz Waldemar (51 volumes) cover the period July 1903-

August 1914; the log of the Prinz Sigismund, December 1908-April 1909. In all likelihood these ships and their logs were seized by the United States Government upon its entrance into World War I and were thereafter confiscated. The logs for each vessel are arranged chronologically.

NEXT-OF-KIN LISTS FROM SHIPS. 1941-42. 27 vols. 5 ft.   126

These lists show next of kin for all officers and enlisted men aboard various classes of Navy vessels. The back of form NAVPERS 134, "Deck Log--Columnar Sheet" was often used for this listing or else separate sheets containing this information were stapled to it. The forms in this series were bound separately in post binders like the ships' logs and were submitted monthly with the logs. The volumes are arranged alphabetically; the lists are arranged by name or symbol of ship within each volume and thereunder by month.

COMMUNICATION "LOGS" AND OTHER RECORDS, 1897-1922

SIGNAL-RECORD BOOKS FROM VESSELS. Sept. 1897-Nov. 1898. 6 vols. 7 in.   127

Miscellaneous "rough" and "smooth" signal books (logs) as follows: rough logs for the U.S.S. Texas and the U.S.S. Eagle; smooth logs for the U.S.S. Brooklyn, the U.S.S. New York, and the U.S.S. St. Paul. They contain entries common to such signal-record books, including times of receiving and sending messages, a brief of the message, names of the sender and receiver, code used, and initials of the signaler. Entries within each volume are chronological by day and thereunder by hour and minute. For later series of signal-record books, see entries 128 and 129.

SIGNAL-RECORD BOOKS FROM VESSELS. 1913-18. 423 vols. 28 ft.   128

Contain copies of Bu. Nav. Form No. 72 or equivalent information. The forms (furnished to vessels in commission after November 4, 1901, in accordance with General Order No. 65) contain notations of the date, time of day message was sent, names of the sender and receiver, and a brief of the message. These books provide a record of all official signals, including those by megaphone and "word-of-mouth." The volumes were sent to the Bureau when they were completed or when the vessels were decommissioned. They are in the following groups: (1) 337 small volumes; (2) 52 large volumes; and (3) 34 incomplete or fragmentary volumes, a few of which are from land lookout posts and other small naval installations. The volumes in groups 1 and 2 are arranged alphabetically by name of ship and thereunder chronologically; the ones in group 3 are unarranged. Entries within each volume are chronological. For volumes containing a later form with the same number but a different title, see entry 129.

COMMUNICATION RECORDS RECEIVED FROM SHIPS AND STATIONS ("COMMUNICATION LOG"). 1917-22. 108 ft.   129

Consist of copies of Form N. Nav. 72, Communication Record, submitted

monthly to the Bureau with the vessel's or station's log sheets. The
forms contain summaries of communications received and sent, including
dispatches, reports, and radio messages. There are records from about
900 vessels, followed by miscellaneous communication records from naval
air stations in France, air squadrons, destroyer squadrons, and other
units. Arranged by ship or station and thereunder chronologically,
those for each year stapled together. For another series containing
comparable forms in bound volumes, see entry 128.

SIGNAL LOG AND CODE BOOKS. 1917-19. 177 vols. 15 ft. 130

These volumes, received from naval and transport vessels and from
signal and naval air stations, contain incoming, outgoing, and intercepted messages typed on forms, copies of ALNAVS or other orders and
instructions, and rough and smooth journals containing informal entries
describing activities at listening, signal, and air stations both within
and without the continental United States. Most of the books are from
vessels, both "name" and "symbol" vessels. Methods of keeping station
logs varied widely. Handwritten, usually of the journal type, they contain brief entries such as "Uneventful," or longer entries giving considerable detail. Some of the logs were kept at isolated spots not
involved in World War I action; others were kept aboard vessels and may
contain information supplementing regular ships' logs. Most of the
foreign stations were located in the British Isles and in France. The
volumes are arranged alphabetically by name of vessel or station (Agam-
Yankton); entries within each volume are chronological. There are a
few indexes to messages sent and received by the U.S.S. Plattsburg. The
volumes described in entry 131 differ little from those in this series
except that they are arranged differently and came in from a single
source.

RADIO LOG, RADIO CODE, AND SIGNAL CODE BOOKS. Mar. 1917-Oct. 1919.
134 vols. 14 ft. 131

These volumes contain mainly typewritten copies of ordinary messages
and translations of code dispatches, with a few summaries of telephone
conversations. The messages were received and sent by the Commander of
the Newport News Division, Cruiser and Transport Force. They are in
about 20 subseries, including: Chief of Staff's Radio Logs, Received and
Sent; ALNAVS; ALATLAN (All Atlantic); Admiral's Radio Logs, Received
and Sent; Flag Secretary's Radio Logs, Received and Sent; Communications
Office Radio Log, Received and Sent; Radio Log or Radio Code, Received
and Sent; and miscellaneous incoming, outgoing, and intercepted messages
not readily identifiable with any naval unit or vessel. Within each
subseries the volumes and their contents are arranged chronologically.
For a similar series of signal log and code books from different sources,
see entry 130.

MUSTER ROLLS, 1860-1956

Bound volumes of muster rolls from naval vessels were submitted as
early as July 1798; those from shore establishments were submitted,

together with payrolls, as early as August 1800. Their submission was made compulsory by an act approved March 2, 1799 (1 Stat. 709), which set forth "rules and regulations . . . for the government of the navy of the United States." Article 1 of the act includes the following paragraphs:

> 8. Whenever a captain shall enter or enlist a seaman, he shall take care to enter on his books, the time and terms of his entering, in order to his being justly paid.
>
> 9. The captain shall, before he sails, make return to the Secretary of the Navy a complete list of all his officers and men, with the time and terms of their entering, and during his cruise or station, shall keep a true account of the desertion or death of any of them, and of the entering of others, and after the expiration of the time for which they were entered, and before any of them are paid off, he shall make return of a complete list of the same, including those who shall remain on board his ship.
>
> 12. Whenever any inferior officer, seaman, or other person, be turned over into the ship of a commander other than the one with whom he entered, he is not to be rated on the ship's books, in a worse quality, or lower degree or station, than he served in the ship he was removed from . . . .
>
> 43. Every officer or other person in the navy, who shall knowingly make or sign a false muster, or procure the making or signing thereof, or shall aid or abet in the same, shall be cashiered and rendered incapable of further employment in the navy service of the United States, and shall forfeit all the pay and subsistence money due to him.

Muster rolls of vessels, July 1798-December 1859, and of shore establishments, August 1800-December 1842, are described in entries 90 and 92 of the Checklist of the Naval Records Collection. Those early rolls are in three forms—bound volumes, loose papers, and booklets that were apparently assembled from dismantled large volumes. For certain vessels of the pre-Civil War period no muster rolls are known to exist; for many others only a few survive. Despite the existence of regulations requiring the submission of muster rolls, commanding officers sometimes did not (or in some instances probably could not) send them in. As a result there are gaps in the early rolls as well as some in the later ones, but with the growing importance of this type of record in claim and benefit cases and the rising records consciousness throughout the Government, regulations governing the submission of muster rolls have been more rigidly enforced.

MUSTER ROLLS OF SHIPS. Jan. 1, 1860-June 9, 1900. 366 vols. 36 ft.

132

In three groups, as follows: (1) January 1, 1860-December 31, 1879, <u>Argosy</u> through <u>Yantic</u>, 208 volumes, arranged alphabetically by name of vessel; (2) April 1, 1880-December 31, 1891, volumes 2-48 (volumes 1, 12, and 23 are missing), arranged chronologically by quarter, therein alphabetically by name of vessel; and (3) January 1, 1892-June 9, 1900, <u>Albatross</u> through <u>Yantic</u>, 113 volumes, arranged alphabetically by name of vessel. The volumes contain printed forms giving, for each person on board, information concerning his enlistment and whether he was entitled to honorable discharge, a personal description, the date he was received on board, and data concerning his transfer, discharge, desertion, or death. Group 2 is indexed alphabetically by name of ship.

MUSTER ROLLS OF SHIPS AND STATIONS, TOGETHER WITH SHIPPING ARTICLES. 1891-1900. 154 vols. 8 ft.

133

These volumes contain printed forms for both muster rolls and shipping articles and are in two groups, as follows: (1) rolls of naval vessels, <u>Adams</u> through <u>Yorktown</u> (135 volumes); and (2) rolls of naval stations, rendezvous (receiving stations), torpedo boats, and vessels of the Coast Signal Service and the Coast and Geodetic Survey, together with a few volumes of separately bound shipping articles (19 volumes). Group 1 is arranged alphabetically by name of ship, thereunder alphabetically by initial letter of name; group 2 is unarranged. The shipping articles in the backs of the volumes of muster rolls are arranged chronologically.

MUSTER ROLLS OF SHIPS AND SHORE ESTABLISHMENTS. ca. Jan. 1898-June 30, 1939. 3,532 vols. 681 ft.

134

This is a numbered series, 1-3541, of bound volumes. Volume 1 begins with the roll of the U. S. Torpedo Boat <u>Plunger</u>; volume 3541 ends with the roll of Naval ROTC, Yale University. Volumes 1225, 1327, 1328, 2327, 2627, 2636, 2639, 2640, 2665, 2668, 2669, and 2679 are missing. Volumes 2624, 2666, and 2975 are duplicates. Rolls from 1898 to about 1930 are arranged by chronological period and thereunder alphabetically by name or type of ship or shore unit. From about 1931 to 1939 the rolls are arranged by chronological period, thereunder in three groups (rolls of vessels, rolls of aviation units, and rolls of shore units), thereunder by type of vessel or unit, and thereunder alphabetically or chronologically or by a combination of the two.

MICROFILM COPIES OF MUSTER ROLLS OF SHIPS, STATIONS, AND OTHER NAVAL ACTIVITIES. Sept. 1, 1939-Jan. 1, 1949. 33,452 rolls.

135

Negative microfilm copies of muster rolls of ships, squadrons and attached units, flotillas, flag complements afloat, stations, aviation squadrons, and minor naval units such as armed guards. In June 1939 the Navy Department discontinued the bound-volume form for muster rolls and began the looseleaf system now in use. About 2 months after this date the project of microfilming the looseleaf muster rolls was begun at the Naval Records Management Center, Arlington, Va. The muster rolls are those from vessels that have been decommissioned and have complete records available. Basic forms (or their equivalents) used by all types of activities submitting muster rolls are:

1. NAVPERS 605a, Quarterly Roll, an alphabetic listing of enlisted personnel attached to a ship, station, or other naval unit, and of reservists on active duty. Submitted quarterly by the commanding officer to the Bureau of Naval Personnel.

2. NAVPERS 605b, Report of Changes, an alphabetic listing, for enlisted personnel, of changes relating to rating, transfers to and from ships and stations, and total complement. Submitted monthly by the commanding officer to the Bureau of Naval Personnel.

3. NAVPERS 605c, Passenger List, lists passengers other than enlisted personnel. Submitted at date of sailing from one port to another, usually by the commanding officer to the Bureau of Naval Personnel.

4. NAVPERS 605d, Recapitulation Sheet, is a summary of all changes, showing totals of men on sick list, total changes in ratings, total man days in brig, and gains or losses through enlistments, reenlistments, and discharges. Submitted with NAVPERS 605a and 605b when ship, station, or other unit was decommissioned.

Muster rolls of vessels and flag complements and other units on vessels are arranged alphabetically by name of vessel or by symbol (LST, FA) and number, and thereunder chronologically; those of aviation units are arranged alphabetically by symbol (AV or AVU for aviation units), thereunder by service (CDS, district squadron), and thereunder chronologically; and those of shore activities (which include aviation units after 1946) are arranged alphabetically by symbol (AMMD, ammunition depots), thereunder by name of place where shore activity was located, and thereunder chronologically.

Several systems of numbering the microfilm rolls have been used. In the earlier one, "120," the number assigned the microfilming project, was followed by the roll number; a straight roll number was then used, and this was finally replaced by a code system. Muster rolls for the 1949-56 period are described in entry 136. For indexes to microfilm copies of muster rolls, see entry 137.

MICROFILM COPIES OF MUSTER ROLLS OF SHIPS, STATIONS, AND OTHER ACTIVITIES. Jan. 1949-Dec. 1956. 1,382 rolls. 136
Negative microfilm copies of muster rolls containing similar information to those described in entry 135. Each activity has been assigned

an 8-digit code number. Three types of personnel reports are included: Daily Personnel Diaries (NAVPERS-501), Reports of Changes (BuPers Report 1080-11), and Quarterly Muster Rolls (BuPers Report 1080-10); they are grouped according to activity rather than by type of form. There are 39 rolls labeled "Misc. Partial Illegibles." Target sheets show the muster rolls to be records of the Personnel Diary and Roster Section, Personnel Accounting System Branch, Personnel Accounting Division. For Indexes, see entry 137.

INDEXES TO MICROFILM COPIES OF MUSTER ROLLS. n.d. 5 ft.   137
The following lists are of considerable value in using the microfilm copies of muster rolls described in entries 135 and 136.

1. 1941-46 (see entry 135):
    (a) Typewritten list of vessels, showing microfilm roll number, name of or symbol and number of vessel, and inclusive dates of muster rolls for each vessel. Arranged alphabetically by name of vessel or by symbol and number.
    (b) Typewritten list of shore establishments. Arranged alphabetically by symbol and type of unit and thereunder either alphabetically by name of establishment or numerically by its number.

2. 1946-48 (see entry 135):
    (a) Card index, in two sections, showing inclusive dates of muster rolls and microfilm roll numbers. The first section, with cards numbered 1-1882, is arranged alphabetically by name of vessel or by symbol and number; the second section is arranged alphabetically by name of activity or by symbol and number.
    (b) Three typewritten lists--two lists of vessels, with entries numbered to correspond with the cards in the first section of the above-mentioned index, and a list of activities, arranged alphabetically. These lists seem to duplicate the information given in the card index described in 2(a) above.

3. 1949-56 (see entry 136):
    (a) Photostat copies of "cardex" type indexes showing names of ships and activities and also related code numbers under which muster-roll information can be found on the microfilm copies. Arranged in four groups for the periods 1949-50, 1951-52, 1953-54, and 1955-56. The microfilm copies are similarly divided.
    (b) Typewritten list covering the 39 rolls of "Misc. Partial Illegibles" mentioned in entry 136. Arranged alphabetically by activity.

CIVIL WAR MUSTER ROLLS. May-July 1861; Apr., May, and Oct. 1863.
    11 vols. 1 in.   138
These muster rolls, in paperbound volumes, were all made at the time

prize vessels were captured. They were probably compiled as a basis for payment of prize money to officers and crews of the capturing vessels. The rolls are as follows: (1) 7 rolls of the U.S.S. Minnesota at the time of capturing the barques Pioneer, General Green, and Sally Magee, and the schooners Iris, Sallie Mears, and Crenshaw, May 17-July 1, 1861; (2) 1 roll of the U.S.S. New Ironsides at the time the schooner Amelia was captured by the U.S.S. Flag, May 8, 1863; (3) 1 roll of the U.S.S. New Ironsides at the time the Sloop C. Routerau was captured by the U.S.S. Powhatan, May 16, 1863; (4) 1 roll of the U.S.S. Sonoma at the time the schooner Clyde was captured, April 14, 1863; and (5) 1 roll of the U.S.S. Vanderbilt at the time the barque Saxon was captured, October 30, 1863. The volumes contain the number, name, rate or rank, and pay of each officer and member of the crew. In two volumes there are sections for a roll of Marine guards. Entries in most volumes are arranged in descending order of man's rank or rating.

RECORDS RELATING TO NAVAL OFFICERS, 1798-1940

Functions relating to naval officers were performed by the Office of the Secretary of the Navy until 1861. At that time the Office of Detail was established in the Secretary's Office to handle the detailing of officers, the number of which increased rapidly after the outbreak of the Civil War. In 1865 the Office of Detail was placed under the Chief of the Bureau of Navigation although it continued under the Secretary's jurisdiction. When its functions were definitely assigned to the Bureau of Navigation in June 1889 the Office was abolished. Records of the Office are described in entries 346-354. Correspondence with and relating to officers has been described in this inventory in various entries under the heading "Correspondence, 1850-1945." Certain records relating to engineers are included in this inventory even though they were maintained at least for a time by the Bureau of Steam Engineering. For practical purposes they may be considered Bureau of Navigation records "by inheritance."

The changes in cognizance over affairs of naval officers produced a scattering of relevant records among a number of collections. Part of the early records remained in the Secretary's Office and are a part of Record Group 80, General Records of the Department of the Navy.[2] Others passed from that Office to the Office of Naval Records and Library and are a part of Record Group 45, Naval Records Collection of the Office of Naval Records and Library.[3] Still other records were taken from rec-

---

[2]National Archives, Preliminary Checklist of the General Records of the Department of the Navy, 1804-1944, p. 20-26. Compiled by James R. Masterson. 1945.

[3]National Archives, Preliminary Checklist of the Naval Records Collection of the Office of Naval Records and Library, 1775-1910, p. 25-29. Compiled by James R. Masterson. 1945.

ords of the Bureau of Navigation and placed in the Naval Records Collection. Where these records are pertinent to the ones described below, a cross-reference is made.

Application, Examination, and Appointment Records, 1838-1940

REGISTERS OF APPLICATIONS. Apr. 1897-Oct. 1917. 16 vols. 2 ft. 139

These volumes register applications that were submitted for appointments as assistant paymaster, boatswain, carpenter, chaplain, civil engineer, professor of mathematics, gunner, machinist, and pharmacist. The entries contain information on applicants already in the Navy or from "Civil Life," including part or all of the following: Name, rating and station (if in service), application number, date of birth, date of first application, approvals of superior officers or others, names of persons recommending applicant, notation concerning permission to take examination, date and result of examination, notation of appointment or other disposition, and remarks. Some volumes are arranged alphabetically by name of officer and some chronologically by date of application; others have no consistent arrangement. Some volumes are indexed alphabetically by initial letter of applicant's name.

RECORD OF APPLICATIONS FOR APPOINTMENTS AS CHAPLAINS, PROFESSORS OF
    MATHEMATICS, AND CIVIL ENGINEERS. Apr. 9, 1902-Oct. 16, 1913.
    1 vol. 3/4 in. 140

Contains entries for each applicant, giving his name, date of birth, place of legal residence, date of application and of its receipt, remarks, and a statement of final action; the jacket number assigned; and names of Congressmen recommending him. Entries are arranged by type of position and thereunder chronologically by date application was received. Indexed by type of position, thereunder alphabetically by initial letter of applicant's name.

RECORD OF APPLICATIONS FOR RATINGS AS ASSISTANT PAYMASTER. Apr. 23,
    1902-May 29, 1913. 1 vol. 3/4 in. 141

Contains entries for each applicant, giving his name, date of birth, place of legal residence, date of application and of its receipt, remarks, and a statement of final action; the jacket number assigned; and names of Congressmen recommending him. Arranged chronologically by date application was received. The volume is indexed alphabetically by initial letter of applicant's name.

RECORD OF APPLICATIONS FOR RATINGS AS MATE. Jan. 29, 1903-Mar. 20,
    1905. 1 vol. 3/4 in. 142

Contains entries for each applicant, giving his name, present rating and location, continuous-service certificate number, date of application, names of officers recommending him, personal data, record of service, "grade" based on his enlistment record, and a notation in red as to whether he was given the new rating. Entries are generally in chronological order by date of application. The volume is indexed alphabetically by name of applicant.

APPLICATIONS FOR APPOINTMENTS. 1875-78; 1886-1917. 53 ft. 143

These applications, together with related correspondence, are for a variety of positions. Most of the papers in this series are stamped with file numbers assigned to the general correspondence of the Bureau, beginning in 1885. They are in 16 subseries, mainly by type of position, as acting assistant and assistant paymaster, paymaster's clerk, assistant engineer, civil engineer, assistant surgeon, professor of mathematics, machinist, warrant machinist, chaplain, carpenter, boatswain, gunner, sailmaker, and acting line officer. The earliest subseries, 1875-78, contains applications for positions of carpenter, gunner, sailmaker, and boatswain. The applications for chaplain are scattered. Some of the subseries are accompanied by examination papers. Arranged mainly by subseries, thereunder unarranged. For registers that may be helpful, see entries 103 and 117; for numerical-record and subject cards that may serve as a guide, see entries 92 and 93.

APPLICATIONS FOR POSITIONS AS VOLUNTEER ACTING PAYMASTERS. 1898.
2 ft. 144

With the letters of application are a few press copies of letters sent to the applicants, letters of recommendation, and miscellaneous enclosures. Arranged alphabetically by name of applicant.

LETTERS OFFERING SERVICES IN THE EVENT OF WAR WITH SPAIN. 1898. 5 ft.
145

Applications for officers' commissions or other ratings from men offering their services in the event of war, together with letters of recommendation and other related correspondence. Part of the correspondence is stamped with the "received" stamp of the Secretary's Office and numbered as part of that Office's correspondence; the remainder is stamped and numbered as part of the correspondence of the Bureau of Navigation. Arranged in part alphabetically by name of correspondent.

APPLICATIONS FOR POSITIONS AS VOLUNTEER ENGINEERS. Feb. 13-Aug. 10,
1898. 2 vols. 9 in. 146

Applications and letters of recommendation received by or referred to the Bureau of Steam Engineering, together with related letters from Congressmen, a few endorsements, and copies of letters sent by the Bureau. Arranged chronologically. The volumes are indexed alphabetically, with references to the classification numbers of the Bureau of Steam Engineering that appear on each letter.

APPLICATIONS FOR NAVAL RESERVE COMMISSIONS. 1938-40. 5 in. 147

Applications for commissions in the Naval Reserve and letters on obtaining such commissions. Arranged alphabetically by initial letter of correspondent's name.

TESTIMONIAL LETTERS CONCERNING ENGINEERS. ca. 1838-77. 27 vols. 8 ft.
148

Testimonial letters, recommendations, and attestations of good character that were addressed to the engineers themselves, to superior officers, to examining boards, and to the Secretary of the Navy. They were sent by officers and private employers and were probably used by examining boards for engineers in determining the fitness of such officers for promotion. They are in three subseries, as follows: (1) testimonials concerning engineers (regular service), ca. 1838-74, 3 volumes; (2) testimonials concerning assistant engineers (regular service), ca. 1843-77, 9 volumes; and (3) testimonials concerning volunteer engineers, ca. 1862-73, 15 volumes. The volumes in each subseries are arranged alphabetically and the correspondence therein is arranged chronologically. The volumes are indexed by initial letter of officer's name.

LIST OF APPLICANTS FOR VOLUNTARY RETIREMENT. 1899-1915. 1 vol. 2 in. 149

This volume, labeled "Partial Key to File Case No. 3," contains names of officers applying for retirement, for each rank up to commander, together with information from their letters requesting such action and a statement of action taken. These applications came under the provisions of section 8 of an act of Congress approved March 3, 1899. The list is arranged by rank, thereunder by year. Indexed in general alphabetically by name of officer.

OFFICERS' PHYSICAL FITNESS REPORTS. 1898-99. 9 in. 150

Filed with the physical fitness reports are a few other documents such as medical reports and related correspondence. Arranged alphabetically by folder heading and thereunder alphabetically by name of officer.

REPORTS OF PHYSICAL EXERCISE AND PHYSICAL EXAMINATION OF OFFICERS. 1909-13. 3 in. 151

This series consists of forms titled "Report of First Quarterly Exercise for Officers" and a few titled "Report of Physical Examination," both having the form number N. Nav. 253. The physical exercise reports were, according to the form, "required by General Orders of the Navy Department." Arranged alphabetically by name of officer.

REPORTS OF EXAMINING BOARDS FOR THE ENGINEER CORPS. Sept. 1, 1849-Dec. 31, 1873. 2 vols. 6 in. 152

Reports of boards convening at navy yards (chiefly the Philadelphia Navy Yard) sent to the Secretary of the Navy, or to officers commanding yards, squadrons, and stations who forwarded them to the Secretary. They give the results of examinations of candidates for engineer positions and of engineers seeking promotions. Arranged by yard or other unit, ashore or afloat, and thereunder chronologically. The volumes are indexed alphabetically by name of person examined. Fair copies of some of these reports are described in entry 153.

FAIR COPIES OF REPORTS OF EXAMINING BOARDS FOR THE ENGINEER CORPS.
   Mar. 14, 1863-Mar. 6, 1875. 1 vol. 2 in.   153
   Fair copies of some of the reports described in entry 152. Arranged chronologically. The volume is indexed by initial letter of name of person examined.

WEEKLY REPORTS OF EXAMINING BOARDS FOR ACTING APPOINTMENTS IN THE
   ENGINEER CORPS. Dec. 6, 1862-Mar. 25, 1865. 2 vols. 6 in.   154
   Form reports containing the following information for each engineer examined: his name, occupation, age, by whom examined, by whom recommended, date his papers were forwarded, to what rank he was recommended, length of his service at sea, length of his service in shops, and remarks. The series includes reports from the Baltimore, New York, and Philadelphia Naval Stations, the New York and Philadelphia Navy Yards, and the Mississippi and West Gulf Blockading Squadrons as well as a few quarterly summaries of grades earned. The reports are arranged by name of yard, station, or squadron, and thereunder chronologically. The volumes are indexed alphabetically by initial letter of name of person examined.

RECORD OF PROCEEDINGS OF NAVAL EXAMINING BOARDS. 1899-1902. 4 ft.   155
   These boards examined candidates for ratings as acting boatswains, boatswains, acting gunners, gunners, acting carpenters, carpenters, and warrant machinists. The records include orders to appear for examinations, examination papers (academic), medical examination papers and statements of medical examiners, and minutes of the boards themselves, which usually contain their decisions as to eligibility of the candidates. Arranged by rating examined for and thereunder chronologically.

JOURNALS AND REPORT BOOKS OF EXAMINING BOARDS FOR THE ENGINEER CORPS
   ("RECORDS AND MINUTES OF EXAMINING BOARDS, ENGINEER CORPS . . .
   REGULAR"). July 8, 1845-Jan. 7, 1870. 5 vols. 1 ft.   156
   These volumes contain reports, minutes of meetings, and copies or briefs of examinations given candidates for admission to or promotion within the Engineer Corps, together with a few transmittal and miscellaneous letters. The first four volumes relate only to regular engineers; the last volume relates also to volunteer engineers. Arranged chronologically. The volumes are indexed alphabetically by name of person examined. Fair copies of a part of this series are described in entry 157.

FAIR COPIES OF RECORDS AND MINUTES OF EXAMINING BOARDS FOR THE ENGINEER
   CORPS. Apr. 20, 1857-May 23, 1870. 5 vols. 8 in.   157
   Fair copies of a part of the records described in entry 156. The two earliest volumes are labeled "Minutes of Examination Boards." Arranged chronologically. All the volumes except the earliest one are indexed alphabetically by initial letter of name of person examined.

LETTERS SENT RELATING TO OFFICERS' APPOINTMENTS, ORDERS, AND RESIGNA-
TIONS ("APPOINTMENTS, ORDERS, AND RESIGNATIONS"). Feb. 1842-Dec.
1895. 47 vols. 9 ft. 158

Fair copies of letters sent by the Secretary of the Navy or by the
Chief of the Bureau of Navigation, with the exception of volume 65,
which is titled "List of Officers Ships and Stations Opened 1st January
1895. Shows Commanding Officers of Ships and Stations from date of Commission or Foundation to 1st January 1895, and all Officers attached on
or subsequent to that date." The volumes in this series are numbered
19-65. Volumes 19-64 are arranged chronologically; volume 65, in general,
by class of ship. Volumes 1-10, presumably beginning with 1798 and ex-
tending to May 1813, have been retained by the Navy Department; and
volumes 11-18, May 1813-February 1842, are in the National Archives as a
part of Record Group 45 (see entry 284 in the Checklist of the Naval
Records Collection). The abstracts of service records described in entry
193 serve as an index to the letters in this series.

CONFIRMATIONS OF APPOINTMENTS OF OFFICERS ("CONFIRMATIONS"). Jan. 5,
1843-Aug. 4, 1909. 10 vols. 2 ft. 159

These volumes contain congressional confirmations of officers' appointments to the Navy and the Marine Corps, signed by the Secretary
or Assistant Secretary of the Senate, that were sent to the White House
and later transferred to the Navy Department. Arranged chronologically.
The volumes are indexed alphabetically by name of officer.

ACCEPTANCES AND APPOINTMENTS ("ACCEPTANCES," "ACCEPTANCES AND OATHS,"
"APPOINTMENTS"). Jan. 10, 1873-Apr. 10, 1889. 12 vols. 3 ft. 160

These volumes contain acceptances and appointments, together with
oaths and articles of agreement, that were sent to the Secretary's Office under covering letter and were at one time a part of that Office's
records. The papers concern officers', paymasters', and ships' clerks,
yeomen, "writers," apothecaries, and others. Arranged chronologically.
The first 10 volumes are indexed alphabetically by name.

RECORD OF APPOINTMENTS OF PAYMASTERS' CLERKS AND YEOMEN. Jan. 1, 1890-
Jan. 4, 1898. 1 vol. 3 in. 161

Contains the following information for each appointee: number (probably an appointment number), name of appointee, dates of acceptance and
oath, name of State or Territory from which appointed, name of person
making appointment, and ship or station to which appointed. Arranged
chronologically; the number sequence follows the chronology. The volume
is indexed alphabetically by initial letter of applicant's name.

RECORD OF ACTION TAKEN ON APPLICATIONS FOR RATINGS AS BOATSWAINS AND
GUNNERS. May 24, 1890-Feb. 1, 1900. 1 vol. 3/4 in. 162

Although this volume is labeled "Bureau of Construction and Repair"
it apparently belongs to Bureau of Navigation records because of its
subject matter. It shows, for each applicant, personal data, service-

record data, information regarding the examination taken by him, and action taken concerning him. Arranged by a serial number. The volume is indexed alphabetically by name, with references to the serial number.

RECORD OF VACANCIES AND PROMOTIONS IN THE ENGINEER CORPS. Mar. 1872-July 1897. 1 vol. 3/4 in.   163

This record, although it may have been begun by the Bureau of Steam Engineering, bridges the period of the 1889 reorganization during which the Bureau of Navigation absorbed most of the personnel functions of other bureaus. It was probably continued or at least was used by the Bureau of Navigation and thus became part of its records. The volume gives names, ranks, explanations of how vacancies were created and names of persons appointed to them, records of promotions, and dates of all such changes. Arranged chronologically. The volume is indexed alphabetically by initial letter of person's name.

RECORD OF PROMOTIONS OF OFFICERS. 1909-20. 4 vols. 9 in.   164

Consists of four volumes, two labeled "Dates" and two labeled "Grades." The volumes marked "Dates" show rank of officer, name, grade he was to be promoted to, effective date of promotion, whom he was to replace ("vice"), date he was qualified, date he was nominated, and date his commission was sent. These two volumes are divided into sections for warrant officers, staff officers, Marine Corps, Medical Corps, and others, with entries under each section made chronologically by effective date of promotion. The volumes marked "Grades" contain information arranged by grade or rank and columnized under such headings as "Date," "Name," "Examination Ordered," "Qualified," "Confirmations," "Commission Sent," and "Receipt." The officers' names appear to have been entered according to date of action. These two volumes also show retirements and occasionally other actions as well as promotions.

Commissions and Warrants, 1844-1936

COMMISSIONS ISSUED TO OFFICERS ("COMMISSIONS," "COPIES OF COMMISSIONS ISSUED IN 19__"). Feb. 3, 1844-Dec. 28, 1936. 124 vols. 32 ft.
   165

Copies of commissions, on printed forms, showing the names of appointing officials and the register numbers. Volumes 1-68 are numbered consecutively (with two volumes 10); the remaining volumes are numbered separately for each year. The first 69 volumes are arranged chronologically, the others alphabetically under each year. Volumes 1-68 and 4 volumes for 1924 are indexed alphabetically by initial letter of officer's name.

WARRANTS ISSUED TO OFFICERS ("WARRANTS"). July 11, 1846-Aug. 14, 1925. 8 vols. 2 in.   166

Copies, on printed forms, of warrants issued to officers. The originals of these warrants were apparently signed at first by the President of the United States and later for him by the Secretary of the Navy.

The warrants are arranged in part chronologically. The volumes are indexed by initial letter of name of officer receiving the warrant.

COMMISSIONS AND WARRANTS ISSUED TO CHIEFS OF BUREAUS, NAVY AGENTS, AND
    ASSISTANT ENGINEERS ("COMMISSIONS AND WARRANTS"). July 12, 1848-
    May 28, 1896. 1 vol. 4 in.   167
    Copies, on printed forms, that are grouped in sections according to the three classes receiving the warrants. The inclusive dates vary with each class. Arranged by type of commission and thereunder chronologically. The volume is indexed alphabetically by initial letter of name of person to whom the commission or warrant was issued. For a volume of commissions and warrants, August 1848-May 1896, issued "mainly to chiefs of bureaus," see entry 47 in the Preliminary Checklist of the General Records of the Department of the Navy, 1804-1944.

COMMISSIONS, DISCHARGES, AND RESIGNATIONS OF SPANISH-AMERICAN WAR OF-
    FICERS. Apr. 1898-Apr. 1899. 4 vols. 1 ft.   168
    These are fair and typewritten copies, on printed forms. Two of the volumes contain copies of commissions; the other two volumes contain copies of discharges and resignations. Arranged alphabetically by name of officer.

COMMISSIONS OF OFFICERS OF THE NAVAL MILITIA OF THE DISTRICT OF COLUMBIA.
    Aug. 12, 1898-Apr. 10, 1917. 1 vol. 2 in.   169
    Fair copies, on printed forms, with a record of discharges and resignations entered in red ink. Arranged chronologically. The volume is indexed alphabetically by initial letter of officer's name.

COMMISSIONS ISSUED TO OFFICERS OF THE NATIONAL NAVAL VOLUNTEERS.
    Jan. 22, 1917-June 8, 1918. 2 vols. 3 in.   170
    Fair copies, on printed forms. They are arranged in general chronologically by date on which the Secretary or the President signed the commission and thereunder alphabetically by initial letter of name of person commissioned. The volumes are indexed alphabetically by name of officer.

Orders and Related Records, 1883-1903

DAILY RECORD OF ORDERS ISSUED TO OFFICERS. July 2, 1883-July 18, 1885.
    1 vol. 2 in.   171
    The entries in this volume of press copies show action taken during the day in connection with officers, under such headings as "Ordered," "Detached," "Revoked," "Resigned," "Promoted," "Placed on Retired List," "Leave," and "Modified." Arranged chronologically. An early register of orders to officers is described in entry 138 of the Checklist of the Naval Records Collection.

TELEGRAMS AND CABLES CONVEYING ORDERS TO NAVAL OFFICERS ("TEL.").
    Nov. 1, 1897-June 27, 1903. 33 vols. 3 ft.   172
    Press copies of orders, some in code, sent by the Secretary of the

Navy and the Chief of the Bureau of Navigation. Arranged chronologically. The volumes are indexed in part alphabetically by name of officer, yard, station, ship, or subject.

ORDERS SENT TO ACTING ENGINEERS DURING THE SPANISH-AMERICAN WAR. May 4, 1898-Apr. 26, 1899. 2 vols. 2 in. <u>173</u>
Fair copies of orders to acting engineers (volunteers). The earlier volume also contains a record of appointment of engineers, April-August 1898. Arranged chronologically. Each volume is indexed alphabetically by initial letter of officer's name.

PRESS COPIES OF LETTERS SENT RECOMMENDING DUTY ASSIGNMENTS FOR ENGINEER OFFICERS ("NAVAL ENGINEERS' NOMINATION BOOK"). Jan. 21, 1895-Aug. 14, 1899. 2 vols. 3 in. <u>174</u>
These letters were sent by the Chief of the Bureau of Steam Engineering to the Office of Detail. It is assumed that these press copies were used by the Bureau of Navigation for its own purposes or were inherited mainly because of their connection with other personnel matters relating to officers. Arranged chronologically. The volumes are indexed alphabetically by initial letter of officer's name.

Identification Records and Photographs, 1862-1939

AGE CERTIFICATES SIGNED BY OFFICERS ("AGES"). Jan. 1862; Oct. 1863. 4 vols. 1 ft. <u>175</u>
These are form letters that were sent by the Office of the Secretary of the Navy to officers and returned by the latter with their attestations and signatures. The certification is in reality to the officer's date of birth rather than to his age. In two groups as indicated by the dates above; therein arranged, in general, alphabetically. Each volume contains an alphabetical name index.

IDENTIFICATION PHOTOGRAPHS OF OFFICERS. 1889-1939. 7 ft. <u>176</u>
This series of 3,300 prints of varying sizes does not include photographs of all Navy officers for the dates indicated. The pictures are in envelopes, most of which are labeled with the name of the officer. Arranged alphabetically by name.

PORTRAITS OF OFFICERS, PASSPORT NEGATIVES, AND COPY NEGATIVES OF CHARTS, MEDALS, TROPHIES, AND VESSELS. 1917-37. 25 ft. <u>177</u>
This series consists of 2,666 glass-plate negatives, 834 nitrate-film negatives, and 900 cut prints--a total of 4,400 items of varying sizes. Included are 143 8" x 10" copy negatives of naval vessels. With the exception of the glass-plate negatives, most of the material is in labeled envelopes. The portraits and passport negatives are arranged alphabetically by name of person; the copy negatives are arranged by category and thereunder alphabetically by name of person or ship.

IDENTIFICATION CERTIFICATES ISSUED TO OFFICERS IN LIEU OF PASSPORTS.
Oct. 1917-Apr. 1921. 9 ft. 178
Copies of the identification certificate (Form N. Nav. 301), or a mimeographed form resembling it, together with photographs (attached), birth certificates, and related correspondence. The forms show the rating held by the officer, the names of places to be visited, a personal description, his fingerprints, his name, a copy of the signature of the Secretary of the Navy, and a serial number. Arranged by number, 1-4217. For a card index to these records, see entry 179.

CARD INDEX TO IDENTIFICATION CERTIFICATES ISSUED TO OFFICERS IN LIEU OF PASSPORTS. 1917-21. 3 ft. 179
These cards show the name of the officer, his rank, and the certificate number. Arranged alphabetically by name of officer. The identification certificates themselves are described in entry 178.

Registers, Rosters, and Records Showing Complements, 1799-1909

Lists of naval, marine, and civil officers of shore establishments (1855-89) and of naval vessels (1861-77) are described in entries 95 and 96, respectively, of the Checklist of the Naval Records Collection. In addition to the registers of officers described below, registers of regular naval officers (1798-1874) and of volunteer naval officers (1861-79) are described in entries 113-130 of the Checklist.

REGISTER OF OFFICERS OF THE NAVY. Mar. 5, 1799-ca. Sept. 25, 1823.
1 vol. 2 in. 180
This volume, labeled "G. Navy Department," contains numbered entries giving the officer's name, a date (apparently that of his commission), and his home State. Arranged by rank, thereunder by entry number. The volume is indexed alphabetically by name of officer, with a reference to the entry number.

"SHIP BOOKS" CONTAINING COMPLEMENTS AND ROSTERS OF OFFICERS ON VESSELS.
Nov. 1834-ca. Sept. 1865. 4 vols. 8 in. 181
Under the name of each vessel, such information as the following is given: class designation of the vessel (as "Columbus 74"), dates of sailings and arrivals, roster of officers, and data on passengers carried. Some entries also include names of enlisted men. The first three volumes are arranged by class of vessel, thereunder by name of vessel, and thereunder chronologically by dates of sailing and return; the last volume, alphabetically by name of ship. The volumes are indexed alphabetically by initial letter of ship's name.

REGISTERS OF OFFICERS OF THE ENGINEER CORPS ("REGISTER"). Apr. 1859-
Aug. 1901. 5 vols. 11 in. 182
Entries give name of the officer, date of warrant, and data listed chronologically concerning his service, with page references to unidentified personnel records. Arranged chronologically by date of appointment.

The volumes are indexed alphabetically by initial letter of officer's name. A similar register for the period 1842-61 is described in entry 115 of the Checklist of the Naval Records Collection.

LISTS OF OFFICERS ASSIGNED TO THE NAVAL OBSERVATORY AND THE NAVAL ACADEMY. Dec. 31, 1865-Dec. 31, 1877. 1 vol. 2 in. 183

These are monthly returns, made part of the time on forms, showing names and ranks of officers. About half the book relates to officers of the Naval Observatory (December 31, 1865-December 31, 1877) and the other half to officers of the Naval Academy (January 1, 1866-February 5, 1870). The returns in each group are arranged chronologically.

REGISTER OF ASSISTANT SURGEONS. Jan. 1876-July 1896. 1 vol. 2 in.
184

Entries contain serial number, name of the assistant surgeon, date of his appointment, State from which he was appointed, date "permitted," and title of his position which is the same for all entries. Arranged by serial number (which was assigned chronologically). The volume is indexed alphabetically by name of appointee. An earlier register of applications for appointment to this position is described in entry 99 of the Checklist of the Naval Records Collection.

LISTS OF OFFICERS. 1878-1909. 43 vols. 7 ft. 185

These volumes are in subseries, as follows: (1) quarterly lists of officers on ships, 1878-1905, 27 vols.; (2) quarterly lists of officers on shore duty, 1895-1909, 13 vols.; and (3) quarterly lists of officers at shore stations, 1907-9, 3 vols. These lists, prepared by commanding officers of ships and stations and forwarded to the Bureau of Navigation, give names and ranks of officers on board, changes since last report, dates of arrival, destination, and other information. Arranged by year, thereunder by name of ship or shore establishment, and thereunder chronologically. The earliest volume in subseries 2 is indexed alphabetically by name of shore establishment.

GUNNERS' REGISTER ("GUNNERS"). 1890-98. 1 vol. 1 in. 186

Contains the usual information found in such registers, one page being reserved for each man. Shown are his name, personal data, continuous-service certificate number, dates of appointments and other service-record information, file numbers of pertinent correspondence, dates of examinations, and actions taken. Unarranged. The volume is indexed in part alphabetically by man's name.

REGISTERS OF PETTY OFFICERS HOLDING PERMANENT APPOINTMENTS. 1893-1902.
3 vols. 7 in. 187

Contain such information as continuous-service certificate number, name of officer, date and place of current enlistment, date of appointment, and notations of reenlistment or discharge. The first volume is arranged by class of officer and thereunder chronologically by date of current enlistment; the second and third volumes are arranged alphabetically by initial letter of officer's name. The earliest volume is indexed alphabetically by initial letter of officer's name.

REGISTER OF COMMISSIONED OFFICERS OF THE AUXILIARY NAVAL FORCE. 1898. 1 vol. 1 in. <u>188</u>

Contains the following information for each officer: his name, rank, date of appointment, register number, place of present duty or station, date of orders, date of reporting for duty, State from which appointed, notation as to whether he was appointed from the Naval Militia, position from which he was appointed, date of discharge, and his home address. Arranged alphabetically by name of officer.

Personnel Jackets and Other Personnel Records, 1900-1925

PERSONNEL JACKETS FOR OFFICERS OF THE NAVAL AUXILIARY SERVICE. 1900-1916. 39 ft. <u>189</u>

These jackets contain such documents as applications to enter the Naval Auxiliary Service, questionnaires, letters of recommendation, oaths of office, and fitness reports, together with related correspondence. Arranged alphabetically by name of officer; regulations for the Naval Auxiliary Service and changes thereto, 1914-17, are at the end of the series. The personnel record cards described in entry 191, although not directly indexing these records, summarize the service records, as do some of the records described in entry 199. For additional personnel jackets for officers in the Naval Auxiliary Service, see entry 190.

PERSONNEL RECORDS FOR OFFICERS AND MEN OF THE NAVAL AUXILIARY SERVICE. 1901-17. 10 ft. <u>190</u>

This series consists of three subseries: (1) folders for officers and enlisted men, containing their applications, letters of recommendation, fitness reports, and related correspondence; arranged alphabetically by name; (2) correspondence of the Supervisor of Naval Auxiliaries, Norfolk, Va., concerning mainly changes in crew personnel of Naval Auxiliary Service vessels; in folders most of which are marked with numerical symbols, 24-49 through 24-749, and arranged in numerical sequence; and (3) personnel folders, one for each officer, arranged alphabetically by name. For other personnel jackets for officers in the Naval Auxiliary Service, see entry 189. For cards and other records summarizing the service of Naval Auxiliary Service officers and enlisted men, see entries 191 and 199.

PERSONNEL RECORD CARDS FOR OFFICERS AND MEN OF THE NAVAL AUXILIARY SERVICE. 1901-17. 6 ft. <u>191</u>

In two groups, one for officers and the other for enlisted men. The cards for officers show the name, address, place and date of birth, rating, date of appointment, file number, application record, name and address of next of kin, and a summary of service. Cards for enlisted men are more detailed and show the name, rating, date of shipment, vessel shipped on, vessel of present service, number on shipping articles, wages per month, term of shipment, place and date of birth, occupation, description, next of kin, name of witnessing officer, date of transfer, date discharged, a notation as to whether the man deserted or died, reason for discharge, recommendation for reshipment, and home address. Within each group the cards are arranged alphabetically by name. There is some duplication between these cards and the summary records described in entry 199.

MICROFILM COPY OF AN INDEX TO OFFICERS' JACKETS ("OFFICER DIRECTORY"). 1913-25. 2 rolls. **192**

These rolls of negative microfilm cover a period for which there are no corresponding officers' jackets in the National Archives. For each officer the index shows the name, rank, location of his file, cross-references to related correspondence, and the jacket number. The entries are arranged by the jacket number or by the file number assigned to the correspondence. The chief value of the index is to provide information as to the location of files. This index may also be of some value in connection with general correspondence for the period 1903-13, described in entry 88, because that series contains letters relating to officers under the original file numbers if the officer was commissioned before 1913.

Records of Service, 1798-1924

ABSTRACTS OF SERVICE RECORDS OF NAVAL OFFICERS ("RECORDS OF OFFICERS"). May 1798-July 1924. 60 vols. 17 ft. **193**

The volumes containing these abstracts are in the following subseries:

1. Volumes (21), designated by the letters A-1 through O-2, cover the period (according to the backstrips) May 1798-December 1893. The early volumes in this subseries contain the date of the officer's appointment, the State from which he was appointed, and the date of termination of his service; later volumes contain, in addition, information relating to his orders, promotions, leave, and retirement. From 1832 the entries are in numbered paragraphs. Volumes A through F are arranged alphabetically by initial letter of officer's name and thereunder chronologically by date of commission; volumes G through O-2 are arranged by rank and thereunder chronologically by date of commission. Volumes designated by the same letter cover the same chronological period.

2. The one volume (1) in this subseries is unlabeled, but it covers the period 1799-1829, these dates representing approximately the earliest dates of the officers' commissions or orders and the latest dates the men were in service. The volume contains numbered paragraphs summarizing the service record of officers of certain ranks and does not fit into either of the other subseries. Arranged by officer's rank and thereunder chronologically by date of his commission.

3. These volumes (38) cover the period February 1829-July 1924, and are numbered. The dates represent approximately the earliest dates of the officers' commissions or orders and the latest dates the men were in service. This subseries consists of the form "Record of Officers, U. S. Navy," which shows the dates of service, name of officer, the time devoted to sea service or "unemployed," and remarks. The names are mainly in chronological order by date of appointment.

Most of the volumes in subseries 1 and 2 are indexed alphabetically by initial letter of officer's name and thereunder by rank; those in subseries 3 are indexed alphabetically by initial letter of officer's name only. Separate index volumes to the third subseries are described in entry 194. Most of the entries in this series show a number in parentheses that is the page number of a volume (of corresponding date) described in entry 158.

INDEXES TO ABSTRACTS OF SERVICE OF NAVAL OFFICERS. Feb. 1829-July 1924.
    2 vols. 4 in.   194

This series consists of one bound volume and one looseleaf notebook of typed sheets, both of which are indexes to subseries 3 of entry 193. In both indexes the name of the officer is given, together with references to the volume and page number of the abstracts. The bound volume appears to cover only volumes 1-13; the typed list covers all 38 volumes. Arranged alphabetically by name of officer.

LETTERS FROM OFFICERS TRANSMITTING STATEMENTS OF THEIR SERVICE.
    June 1842-Dec. 1844. 2 vols. 5 in.   195

These letters were submitted in compliance with the provisions of a directive from the Secretary of the Navy. Some of the communications are merely transmittal letters for the printed forms that are described in entry 72 of the <u>Checklist of the Naval Records Collection</u>, but others present supplementary data. Since many of the letters are from prominent officers, the statements of service are valuable for biographical details and for the history of the Navy. Unarranged.

RECORDS OF SERVICE OF OFFICERS. n.d. 3 in.   196

According to a form letter from the Chief of the Bureau of Navigation and Office of Detail, these records may have been compiled during the years 1866-67. They contain summaries of service of officers who served in the War of 1812, the Mexican War, and the Civil War. Most of the records cover Civil War service and show the officer's name, station, date of birth and other personal data, kinds and dates of commissions, inclusive dates of service, types of boards served on, wounds received, and battles engaged in. Arranged alphabetically by name of officer.

LISTS OF NAVAL OFFICERS AND RECORDS OF THEIR SERVICE ("RECORD OF SERVICE"). Dec. 1884-Jan. 1891. 1 vol. 1 in.   197

The first 95 pages of this volume of press copies contain lists of officers serving at navy yards. The remainder of the volume contains lists of other naval officers, service histories of individual officers, and miscellaneous personnel information. The lists of officers are unarranged; the service records are arranged chronologically. Indexed alphabetically by initial letter of officer's name.

RECORD OF SERVICE OF TEMPORARY OFFICERS IN THE SPANISH-AMERICAN WAR. 1898-99. 1 vol. 3 in. 198

This volume contains forms titled "Record of Temporary Officers, U. S. Navy," showing dates of service; name of officer; orders and transfers; time spent in sea service, on shore, and "unemployed"; and remarks. Arranged in general by date of appointment.

RECORDS SUMMARIZING SERVICE OF OFFICERS AND MEN OF THE NAVAL AUXILIARY SERVICE. 1901-17. 8 ft. 199

Consist of pink slips, each of which records briefly the individual's service record. They were prepared in the Bureau of Navigation from information taken from ships' logs. There is some duplication between these slips and the personnel record cards described in entry 191, but this series contains entries for some men and officers for whom cards or other personnel records are missing. Each slip contains a man's name, a statement of his rating or work, name of his ship, and dates of his entry into and departure from the Naval Auxiliary Service. Arranged alphabetically by man's name.

Other Records Relating to Officers, 1863-92

REPORTS ON OFFICERS UNDER INSTRUCTION AND ARREST ON THE U.S.S. SAVANNAH, NEW YORK NAVY YARD. Jan. 1863-Sept. 1864. 4 in. 200

These weekly reports, made to the Secretary of the Navy, show the name of the officer, his rank, type and location of duty assignment, scale of comparative proficiency (rating), and a schedule of daily exercises or drills. Unarranged.

REPORTS OF LINE AND STAFF OFFICERS. 1864-70; 1875. 2 ft. 201

Consist principally of copies of Form 26, "Report of Line Officers Attached to the U.S.S. _____, Commanded by _____, for the quarter ending _____, 18__," and of Form 27, which is similar except that "Staff" is substituted for "Line" in the title. Both forms show the name of the officer, his rank, impressions as to his general and special qualifications, languages spoken, remarks, and recommendations. The forms were received from naval vessels, stations, and yards, including some from such noted vessels as the Constellation and the Constitution. The series also includes a few reports on prisoners confined, quarterly returns of punishments, and other subjects. Arranged by station, yard, or vessel.

LETTERS OF RESIGNATION RECEIVED FROM OFFICERS. Feb. 1878-Nov. 1886. 1 vol. 2 in. 202

Letters addressed to the Secretary of the Navy, together with endorsements indicating the rejection or acceptance of the resignations. Apparently some or all of the requests were acted on by the Detail Division of the Secretary's Office, since many are stamped as received by that Division. Arranged chronologically. Indexed by initial letter of officer's name. An earlier series of resignations is described in entry 65 of the Checklist of the Naval Records Collection. Related series of resignations are described in entries 76 and 85 of the Checklist.

MONTHLY REPORTS ON OFFICERS, NONCOMMISSIONED OFFICERS, MUSICIANS, AND PRIVATES OF THE U. S. MARINE CORPS. 1889-92. 1 in.   203

These form reports contain information relating to stations, allowances for each grade or rating, and totals. Arranged chronologically by month and year.

RECORDS RELATING TO ENLISTED MEN, 1846-1943

Until 1885 the principal reporting activities on enlistments were performed by recruiting stations, receiving ships, and naval vessels other than receiving ships.

Recruiting stations (or rendezvous) were located in certain of the larger cities and served those cities and nearby towns and rural areas. They kept a record of each man enlisted and reported weekly to the Navy Department by means of rendezvous reports (see entries 216-220). These reports were supplemented by composite shipping articles (see entries 358-360), a kind of contract between the enlisted men on board and the commanding officer (representing the Navy Department) to which each man affixed his signature. These shipping articles had the same force as the individual shipping articles now in use and were in other respects similar to them, except that information concerning next of kin and marital status was not required at that time.

Receiving ships were located at coastal cities where they could conveniently supply men to vessels of the fleets. Like the recruiting stations, they also made weekly reports to the Navy Department regarding the enlisted men who were received, transferred, or discharged, or who deserted or died during the week covered by the report. The weekly reports from receiving ships are described in entry 222.

Commanding officers of regular naval vessels were authorized to make enlistments on board their ships as the occasion demanded, from men of any nationality, race, or religion. These enlistments were kept separate from those made at recruiting stations and receiving ships. In most instances the enlistments made on board vessels were for the duration of a particular cruise and might terminate (1) when that cruise was completed, (2) when the enlistment term of the man was completed, or (3) when he was no longer needed.

Naval service of enlisted men during the Civil War period has occasioned more research than has service for any other period. This is due in part to the number of benefits available to men who could establish valid claims to them, in part to the complex nature of the records, and in part to errors in the records themselves. Many erroneous entries of desertions appeared in the records at the close of the war, entries made probably as a result of systematic demobilization procedures. Many men went home, for example, because their commanding officers told them their services were no longer required. Some men went on leave without explicit orders to return and failed thereafter to report to naval authorities. These men were technically deserters but many who were not intentionally so were afterward declared to have been separated under honorable conditions.

On January 1, 1885, the present system of preparing a separate service record, or "jacket," for each enlisted man was inaugurated. These and most other records pertaining to enlisted men have been retained by the Bureau of Naval Personnel. However, a sufficient quantity of records, both earlier and later, has been transferred to the National Archives to be of considerable value in searching the service records of enlisted men.

Series of records described in this inventory that are important in this searching are: keys to enlistment returns, entries 224 and 225; microfilm copy of index to muster rolls, rendezvous reports, and other personnel records, entry 206; muster rolls, entries 132-138; logbooks of ships and stations, entries 118-126; personnel records of officers and men of the Naval Auxiliary Service, 1901-17, entries 190, 191, and 193; and records relating to enlisted men who served during the period 1842-85, entry 204. The keys to enlistments serve a purpose somewhat similar to personnel jackets except that jacket files cover longer periods of time. The microfilm copy of the index, which contains data assembled from muster rolls and other records, shows the man's service in subseries that are in chronological order. The logs often include personnel changes, injuries, and other details lacking in other records.

RECORDS RELATING TO ENLISTED MEN WHO SERVED IN THE NAVY BETWEEN 1842
    AND 1885. 1885-1941. 340 ft. 204

These are folded papers that have been assembled and put into envelopes, or "jackets," one jacket for each enlisted man. The papers include old records of the Bureau of Equipment and Recruiting as well as correspondence of the Bureau of Navigation, particularly of the Muster Roll and Record Section of the Enlisted Personnel Division. Correspondence was apparently collected on each enlisted man who had served in the Navy between 1842 and 1885 and who afterward (between 1885 and 1941) made application for pension, filed any type of claim, asked for discharge documents or service records, or who wanted some other benefit such as admission to the Naval Home at Philadelphia. The jackets contain letters received, copies of letters sent, endorsements, applications for certificates of honorable discharge or for copies of other documents, certificates of medical officers or of special boards convened to examine applicants for pensions or other benefits, legal papers such as affidavits and powers of attorney, and similar items. The jackets are arranged alphabetically by name of enlisted man; contents of the jackets are arranged in part chronologically.

CORRESPONDENCE JACKETS ON ENLISTED MEN. 1904-43. 6 ft. 205
These jackets are for those enlisted men for whom no regular jackets had been made, for Naval Home beneficiaries, and for United States marines. The correspondence, relating mainly to verification of service in connection with applications for benefits, claims against the Navy Department, and other requests, consists of letters received by the Bureau of Navigation and copies of letters sent, together with such types of enclosures as applications, affidavits, permits to enter the Naval Home, certificates and reports of examination from medical officers, and copies of discharges. A small part of the correspondence pertains to retirement. With the exception of this part, the records are arranged alphabetically by name of enlisted man.

MICROFILM COPY OF AN INDEX TO RENDEZVOUS REPORTS, MUSTER ROLLS, AND
    OTHER PERSONNEL RECORDS. 1846-84. 67 rolls. 206
The card records from which these rolls of positive microfilm were made have been destroyed. The films are in four separately numbered subseries as follows: (1) those for periods before and after the Civil War, 32 rolls; (2) those for the Civil War period, 31 rolls; (3) those for armed guard personnel, 3 rolls; and (4) those for the Naval Auxiliary Service, 1 roll. Each card microfilmed showed the man's name, the date of his enlistment, the rendezvous, a page reference to the "Rendezvous Reports" or other records concerning enlisted personnel, and a brief record of his service. Within each subseries the records are arranged alphabetically by name of enlisted man. For weekly returns of enlistments at naval rendezvous, see entry 219; and for muster rolls, see entry 132.

RECORD CARDS FOR ENLISTED MEN WHO SERVED DURING THE FIRST WORLD WAR
    ("STATE CARDS"). 1917-19. 437 ft. 207
Each card shows the enlisted man's name, service number, place and date of his enrollment or enlistment, age and rating at enlistment, home address (including county and State), places and dates of service and ratings for each period, total days of service, place and date of discharge, and rating at time of discharge. Most of the cards are arranged alphabetically by State, with sections at the end for Guam, Hawaii, the Philippines, Puerto Rico, and Samoa, and thereunder alphabetically by man's name.

REGISTER OF PETTY OFFICERS, SEAMEN, AND OTHERS RECEIVED ON BOARD RECEIVING SHIPS AT THE NAVAL RENDEZVOUS AT BALTIMORE. 1855-69. 1 vol. 3 in. 208
This register is for the receiving ships Ontario, Alleghany, and

<u>Fortune</u>. It gives man's name, rank, enlistment data, date of appearance on board, personal description, trade or occupation, name of last ship served on, place of birth, wounds or infirmities contracted in service, and remarks concerning transfer. Entries are arranged by name of receiving ship and thereunder chronologically by date of man's enlistment.

RECORDS RELATING TO MANPOWER REQUIREMENTS FOR THE NAVAL SERVICE. 1892-97. 1 vol. 2 in. 209

Press copies of estimates, memoranda, and letters concerning men required for naval service. Some of these communications are addressed to the Secretary of the Navy; others were apparently for intrabureau information and use. The volume also includes a list of men required. Arranged chronologically.

RECORD CARDS FOR RECIPIENTS OF MEDALS, BADGES, BARS, AND PINS ISSUED BY THE NAVY DEPARTMENT. 1899-1910. 6 ft. 210

Give the recipient's name, continuous-service certificate number, date and kind of award, and ship served on, often with a reference to the Bureau's general correspondence, 1889-1913 (described in entry 88). In that series there is usually a BuNav Form 28, cross-reference slip, and a copy of the form letter transmitting the badge. Where the man was stationed when he received the award determines which series of press copybooks contains another press copy of this transmittal letter. Usually, however, the reference is to the series described in entry 69 or in entry 70. Arranged alphabetically by name of recipient.

STATISTICS RELATING TO ENLISTMENTS. Jan. 5, 1907-Jan. 1, 1910. 1 vol. 3/4 in. 211

Weekly and monthly statistical tabulations of enlistments at recruiting stations, on vessels, and by recruiting parties, together with tables of per capita costs of enlistments. Arranged alphabetically by name of station, vessel, or party and thereunder chronologically; the tables are arranged chronologically. The index by station, vessel, and recruiting party does not apply to the tables.

REPORTS OF REJECTION OF APPLICANTS FOR ENLISTMENT IN THE NAVY. 1908-18. 1 ft. 212

Consist mainly of copies of Form N. Nav. 54, a report of rejection, giving enlistment data, a statement of service, and a description of the applicant. On the back of the form are endorsements of medical officers, a waiver of physical disqualifications (if any), and a statement as to whether the applicant was enrolled or finally rejected. Unarranged.

Registers and Lists of Recruits, 1861-73

INDEX TO PERSONNEL ON THE RECEIVING SHIP <u>OHIO</u>. ca. 1861-65. 2 vols. 2 in. 213

These volumes contain an alphabetical index to the ship's company, supernumeraries, and recruits, and show numbers that are probably service numbers. The entries are arranged alphabetically by type of personnel, such as firemen, coal heavers, and boys, and thereunder alphabetically by initial letter of name. For a register of recruits on this ship at a later date, see entry 214.

REGISTER OF RECRUITS ON THE RECEIVING SHIP OHIO. Aug. 1866-June 1873. 1 vol. 3 in. <u>214</u>
Contains for each recruit received at Boston, Mass., the following information: personal description, occupation, date of enlistment, and name of ship to which assigned. The entries are arranged chronologically. Pages 2-29 are missing. For an index to personnel on this ship at an earlier date, see entry 213.

LISTS OF RECRUITS ENLISTED FOR SERVICE DURING THE CIVIL WAR. Feb. 1864-June 1865. 36 vols. 2 ft. <u>215</u>
These are lists of recruits, mainly substitutes and volunteers, who were enlisted at Baltimore, Boston, Brooklyn, Cairo, Chicago, Cincinnati, Jersey City, and New York. The lists from different cities are for varying periods, but they are within the overall dates given in the series title. There is also some variation in both form and content of the lists. The volumes are arranged alphabetically by place of enlistment and thereunder chronologically.

Enlistment Returns, Changes, and Reports, 1846-1942

DESCRIPTIVE LISTS OF MEN ENTERED AT THE NAVAL RENDEZVOUS AT BALTIMORE. Jan. 1846-Feb. 1852. 1 vol. 1 in. <u>216</u>
One page at the beginning of the volume contains a list of men shipped from Baltimore in 1844 and 1845. The remainder of the volume is in columnized form and shows year, name, rating, pay, bounty, term of service, place of birth, personal description, "securities" (presumably names of persons vouching for the man enlisted), and remarks. Arranged chronologically. There is no other volume containing the same type of information before the beginning of weekly returns of enlistments at naval rendezvous (entry 219) in 1855; it seems likely, however, that the first three volumes of the keys to and registers of enlistment returns, 1846-54 (entry 224), were compiled from this and similar volumes that are missing.

RECORD OF SUBSTITUTES ENLISTED AT THE NAVAL RENDEZVOUS AT BOSTON. June 7-30, 1864. 1 vol. 1/4 in. <u>217</u>
This volume contains printed forms giving the following information: name of recruit and date, place, and term of enlistment. Entries are in general arranged chronologically.

RECORD OF VOLUNTEERS ENLISTED AT THE NAVAL RENDEZVOUS AT BOSTON. July 1-Dec. 30, 1864. 1 vol. 1/4 in. <u>218</u>
This volume contains the same information as the one described in entry 217. Entries are in general arranged chronologically.

WEEKLY RETURNS OF ENLISTMENTS AT NAVAL RENDEZVOUS ("ENLISTMENT RENDEZ-
VOUS"). Jan. 6, 1855-Aug. 8, 1891. 110 vols. 14 ft. 219
These volumes contain printed forms giving the following information:
name of recruit, date and term of enlistment and rating, previous naval
service, usual place of residence, place of birth, occupation, and personal description, including permanent marks or scars. On the back of
the form is a statistical recapitulation covering the week reported or,
at later dates, shipping articles. The forms are arranged chronologically by week; returns from all rendezvous for each week are usually
bound together. For keys to and registers of enlistment returns, see
entry 224.

WEEKLY RETURNS OF CHANGES, TRANSFERS, AND DISCHARGES FROM RECRUITING
STATIONS, RECEIVING SHIPS, AND NAVAL RENDEZVOUS ("RECRUITING RENDEZVOUS"). Apr. 1898-June 30, 1902. 10 vols. 2 ft. 220
These volumes contain copies of Bureau of Navigation Form No. 2,
"Return of Changes on board the United States Receiving Ship _____
at _____ for the week ending Saturday, _____, _____."
The first page of this form gives information on men received from other
vessels or stations and the second and third pages, information on those
"transferred, discharged, etc." Each volume, except the earliest, covers
a half year. The returns are arranged by city where rendezvous, recruiting station, or receiving ship was located and thereunder by week; all
reports from a given location are bound together in each volume.

QUARTERLY RETURNS OF ENLISTMENTS ON VESSELS. Apr. 1866-Aug. 1891.
43 vols. 6 ft. 221
These volumes contain printed forms (No. 14 or its earlier equivalent) giving name of recruit; date, place, and term of enlistment;
rating; previous naval service; usual place of residence; place of birth;
age; occupation; and personal description, including permanent marks or
scars. The volumes are arranged by year, sometimes more than one to a
year. Within volumes the returns are arranged by number of the return
and thereunder by quarter. If more than one return was received from
the same vessel the returns are bound together, provided they do not
extend into the next year. For keys to and registers of enlistment
returns, see entry 224.

WEEKLY RETURNS OF RECRUITS ON RECEIVING SHIPS ("RECEIVING SHIP,"
"R. S. RETURNS"). Jan. 6, 1855-June 28, 1902. 143 vols. 19 ft.
222
These volumes contain weekly reports of changes affecting recruits
on receiving ships, including statistics as to the number of recruits
on board, deaths, desertions, discharges, apprehensions, surrenders,
and transfers. Names of recruits, with information as to their naval
service, are also given. The reports are arranged chronologically by
year, thereunder by week, and thereunder by station at which the receiving ship was located; names entered under the various headings are

mainly in alphabetical order. For keys to and registers of enlistment returns, see entry 224. For other reports of changes, see entry 223.

RETURNS OF CHANGES ON BOARD RECEIVING SHIPS ("REPORTS OF CHANGES"). May 13-Dec. 31, 1902. 6 vols. 9 in. 223

These volumes contain weekly reports submitted by vessels and stations other than those whose reports are described in entry 222. The reports, on printed forms, contain the following information: name, rating, character of appointment, number of continuous-service certificate, dates of beginning and expiration of enlistment, date received on ship, name of vessel received from, and remarks as to transfer, discharge, desertion, or death. The reports are arranged by ship, thereunder chronologically, and thereunder by initial letter of man's name. For keys to and registers of enlistment returns, see entry 224.

KEYS TO AND REGISTERS OF ENLISTMENT RETURNS. June 1846-Dec. 1902. 91 vols. 13 ft. 224

Most of these volumes are labeled "Key to Enlistment Returns." From 1861 to 1891 a parallel series of "Registers to Enlistments" was maintained and these volumes were interfiled with the "Keys." For the period 1892-1902 only the "Registers" exist. Both sets of volumes (57 of "Keys" and 34 of "Registers") contain names of men enlisting at rendezvous or on board vessels, enlistment data, and a summary of service. The "Keys" are in volumes according to enlistments made at rendezvous and those made on vessels. If enlistments were made at rendezvous the page references are to the Weekly Returns of Enlistments at Naval Rendezvous (entry 219). If enlistments were made on board vessels the references are to the Quarterly Returns of Enlistments on Vessels (entry 221). The "Registers" through 1869 contain page references to the Weekly Returns of Enlistments at Naval Rendezvous but apparently none to the Quarterly Returns of Enlistments on Vessels. Except for four volumes of incomplete registers for 1861, the volumes of keys and registers are arranged in one series chronologically by year (with some duplication of dates between "Keys" and "Registers") and thereunder by alphabetical section. Within the volumes entries are arranged alphabetically by initial letter of enlistee's name and thereunder chronologically. The main series of "returns" indexed by these volumes are those described in entries 219 and 221. The lists described in entry 216 were apparently the basis for compiling the first three volumes of registers in this series.

KEYS TO MISCELLANEOUS ENLISTMENT RETURNS. 1861-1915. 3 vols. 225

These volumes are similar to those described in entry 224. The overlapping in dates suggests that this series was maintained parallel to a part of that series. The volumes consist of forms containing columns for enlistee's name, source of information concerning his enlistment, and remarks giving such data as the vessel to which man was attached and the date of his discharge. The volumes are arranged in alphabetical order; within each volume the names are arranged alphabetically. The enlistment returns to which these volumes are a key have not been found, but the enlistment information they contain is complete enough to be of value.

REPORTS OF ENLISTMENTS AT NAVY RECRUITING STATIONS. 1903-42. 376 vols. 101 ft. 226

These are daily or weekly reports on Form N. Nav. 4, "Report of Enlistments," which was also used for enlistments at other types of stations and shore establishments as well as on receiving ships. The reports, in general, contain the enlistee's serial or service number, name, a notation as to whether he was enrolled or enlisted, date of enlistment, rating, information relating to his discharge, and the branch of service (later displaced by a column giving the name of vessel or station to which he was transferred). On the backs of the forms are statistical summaries on applicants rejected, enrolled, and enlisted. These volumes are of use in checking enlistment claims of men seeking pensions or other benefits. The early volumes are arranged by calendar year and the later ones by fiscal year, thereunder alphabetically by station. For keys to and registers of enlistment returns before 1903, see entries 224 and 225.

REPORTS OF ENLISTMENTS AT RECEIVING SHIPS, TRAINING STATIONS, HOSPITALS, NAVAL STATIONS, AND NAVAL DISTRICTS. Jan. 1, 1913-June 30, 1926. 39 vols. 12 ft. 227

These reports are on Forms N. Nav. 4, "Report of Enlistments," and N. Nav. 9, "Monthly Report of Enlistments." They are arranged in the following subseries by type of activity reporting: (1) receiving ships and training stations, Jan. 1913-June 1926, 13 volumes; (2) hospitals and naval stations, Jan. 1913-June 1926, 15 volumes; and (3) naval districts, Dec. 1920-June 1926, 11 volumes. Some of the reports for naval districts are bound in the last volume of subseries 1. The series also includes a few reports of enlistments from yards as well as the enrollments, transfers, and discharges of units of the Naval Reserve. Subseries 1 and 2 are arranged by fiscal year, thereunder alphabetically by ship, hospital, or station, and thereunder by week or month; subseries 3 is arranged by fiscal year, thereunder by district, and thereunder by day or week.

REPORTS OF ENLISTMENTS ON VESSELS. 1903-26. 110 vols. 25 ft. 228

These reports are on Forms N. Nav. 4, "Report of Enlistments," N. Nav. 4-B, "Report of Enlistments on Cruising Vessels," and N. Nav. 9, "Monthly Report of Enlistments." These forms contain substantially the same information: the serial number, name, rating, type of discharge, place of first examination, date of enlistment, and name of vessel to which transferred. The volumes are arranged chronologically by calendar or fiscal year, thereunder alphabetically by name or symbol of ship, and thereunder chronologically by week or month. For an earlier series of quarterly returns of enlistment on vessels, see entry 221.

REPORTS OF ENLISTMENTS ON CRUISERS. Jan.-Dec. 1903. 1 vol. 2 in.
229

These reports, submitted monthly by cruisers, are on Form N. Nav. 4, "Report of Enlistments." They contain the following information on men reenlisting: serial number, name, rating, type of discharge, and date of enlistment. Arranged alphabetically by name of ship and thereunder chronologically.

REPORTS OF ENLISTMENTS IN THE NAVAL RESERVE. Jan. 1917-June 1919.
28 vols. 3 ft.
230

Forms N. Nav. 370 (weekly) and N. Nav. 371 (monthly) submitted by the Naval Reserve or such divisions thereof as the Fleet Naval Reserve and the Auxiliary Naval Reserve. The forms give the following information for receiving or other ships and shore installations: serial number, name, rating, type of action (such as enrollment, transfer, or discharge), date of action, and remarks. Arranged by calendar or fiscal year, thereunder by place of enrollment, district, receiving or other ship, or station, and thereunder by week or month.

REENLISTMENTS UNDER CONTINUOUS-SERVICE CERTIFICATES AND WITHIN 4 MONTHS
OF DISCHARGE. 1905-15. 3 vols. 3 in.
231

This record, kept in pencil, contains such information as name, rate, serial number, date of reenlistment, and dates of awards of medals, pins, and bars. Arranged alphabetically by initial letter of name.

Continuous-Service Certificates, 1865-99

CONTINUOUS-SERVICE CERTIFICATES OF ENLISTED MEN. June 22, 1865-Sept. 22, 1899. 55 ft.
232

These certificates are attached to and enclosed within leather folders or wrappers evidently intended as a personal record for the enlisted man to carry with him. For each man the following information is shown: name, date of entry for pay, vessels on which service was performed, rating, professional qualifications, dates of transfer to and discharge from vessels, character of discharge, age, description, health record, pay officer's certificate, and dates of reenlistments. The man's name and service number appear on each wrapper and serve as a label. The certificates are arranged alphabetically by name of enlisted man.

Records Concerning Discharges and Desertions, 1882-1920

INDEX TO CERTIFICATES OF DISCHARGE ("INDEX TO DISCHARGES"). 1882.
1 vol. 1/2 in.
233

This volume contains the names of those to whom certificates of discharge were issued and page references to records that have not been identified. Arranged alphabetically by name of man discharged. The information in the volume is of some value to searchers of service records.

INDEX TO APPLICATIONS FOR DISCHARGE AND HONORABLE DISCHARGES ("APPLICATIONS FOR CERTIFICATES OF DISCHARGE"). Dec. 1890-May 1894. 3 vols. 10 in.   234

These volumes contain the name of each man discharged, the date his application was received, name of person to whom it was referred, the date of discharge certificate, name of person to whom it was addressed, and dates of enlistment and discharge. All volumes contain references in red ink to press copies of letters sent that fall within the limiting dates of this series (see various entries describing press copies of letters sent, particularly entry 2). Arranged alphabetically within each volume by name of man discharged.

INDEX TO CERTIFICATES OF DISCHARGE ISSUED DURING THE PERIOD 1889-90 FOR DISCHARGES MADE DURING AND IMMEDIATELY AFTER THE CIVIL WAR ("CERTIFICATES SENT"). 1889-90. 1 vol. 2 in.   235

Shows name of the man to whom a certificate of discharge was issued, dates of enlistment and discharge, home address, and serial number of discharge certificate. The discharge certificates for the dates covered by this index have not been identified, but the volume in itself has some service-record value. Arranged in general alphabetically by name of man discharged.

INDEX TO CERTIFICATES OF DISCHARGE ISSUED DURING THE PERIOD 1891-94 FOR DISCHARGES MADE DURING AND IMMEDIATELY AFTER THE CIVIL WAR. 1891-94. 1 vol. 1 in.   236

The certificates of discharge recorded here were issued under authority of an act of Congress approved April 14, 1890. This volume contains the same type of information as the volume described in entry 235 except that these discharges were for men who had enlisted under various names or aliases. Arranged in general alphabetically by name of man discharged.

INDEX TO CERTIFICATES OF DISCHARGE ISSUED FROM FEB. 10 TO JUNE 30, 1896. 1/2 in.   237

This volume gives the file numbers for applications for certificates of discharge that were filed in the general correspondence of the Bureau described in entry 88. Arranged alphabetically by name of man discharged.

RECORD OF CERTIFICATES OF DISCHARGE ISSUED UNDER AN ACT OF CONGRESS APPROVED AUG. 14, 1888. 1889-1901. 1 vol. 1 in.   238

Gives the name of the man to whom a discharge certificate was sent, a brief of his enlistment and service record, the date his discharge was sent, and references to the general correspondence of the Bureau (see entry 88). Arranged alphabetically by initial letter of name.

RECORD OF DISCHARGES AND DISENROLLMENTS IN THE NAVAL RESERVE. 1917-20. 1 vol. 2 in.   239

Shows the name, rating, place and date of discharge or disenrollment, and reason for such action. Arranged alphabetically by initial letter of name.

DESCRIPTIVE LISTS OF DESERTERS ("DESERTERS"). Apr. 26, 1902-Dec. 23, 1911. 32 vols. 3 ft. 240

These are press copies of Bureau of Navigation Form 65-B, "Descriptive List of Deserters," that were sent to chiefs of police and detectives. They contain a personal description, enlistment data, an offer of reward for delivery of the deserter, and information relating to the procedure for obtaining reimbursement from the Government for transportation of the deserter to the place of delivery. Arranged chronologically. The volumes are indexed by initial letter of deserter's name.

RECORDS RELATING TO NAVAL APPRENTICES, 1838-97

The naval apprentice system, revived in 1864 by Secretary of the Navy Welles under authority of an act of March 2, 1837, was the first personnel matter to be placed in charge of the Bureau of Navigation. Its object was to supply the Navy with disciplined and better instructed seamen and to free the Navy of its dependence upon the merchant marine. Although apprentices had been enlisted under the same act in 1837 and 1855, no actual training system was set up until 1864. By 1867 the Sabine, the Portsmouth, and the Saratoga, old sailing vessels, were in commission as apprentice ships. Following the passage of an act of June 17, 1868, that limited the number of enlisted men and apprentices to 8,500, it was necessary to reduce the number of apprentices to the capacity of one ship, the Saratoga. Most of the apprentices hoped to pass the examinations for admission to the Naval Academy and so become officers. The annual examination for the admission of 10 boys out of about 500 doomed most of them to disappointment. The large number of desertions that followed resulted in the failure of the apprentice system.

During the years following the Civil War the number of the Navy's ships and personnel decreased markedly. The ships were mainly those left over from a bygone era, and no provision was made by Congress for replacing them with modern steel ships until 1883. The service was unattractive, particularly in those days when the West was offering high adventure. As a result the crews of naval vessels had more foreign seamen than American. This situation became a matter of concern to officers like Capt. Stephen B. Luce, who advocated the establishment of a training system as a means of providing seamen for both the Navy and the merchant marine.

Another apprentice training system was set up pursuant to a Navy Department circular of April 8, 1875, providing, by authority of the act of March 2, 1837, for the enlistment of boys between the ages of 16 and 18 for service until they reached the age of 21. The training was designed merely to fit the boys to be sailors, so the mistake of giving them hope of becoming officers was avoided. Supervision of the apprentice system was placed under the Bureau of Equipment and Recruiting, which since its creation had had charge of the enlistment of men for the Navy. (For records of that Bureau relating specifically to apprentices, see entries 360, 373, and 374.) The apprentices received their first instruction--and later made training cruises--on training ships stationed at one of the large Atlantic coast ports: the Minnesota at New York, the Constitution at Philadelphia, the Monongahela at Baltimore, and the Saratoga at Norfolk. When the boys were transferred to cruising vessels of the Navy, favorable reports were received from officers concerning them. On May 12, 1879, when there were 945 boys serving as apprentices, an act of Congress was approved authorizing the annual enlistment of 750 boys between the ages of 15 and 18 to serve until they were 21. Immediate measures were taken for their recruitment.

The first permanent training station for apprentices was established at Coasters Harbor Island, off Newport, R. I., on June 4, 1883, and, with the training ships, it was under the supervision of the Bureau of Equipment and Recruiting. This island had been ceded by the State of Rhode Island to the United States on March 2, 1881, for use as a training station. In that year it became the headquarters of the Apprentice Training Squadron, which had been established under the command of Commodore Stephen B. Luce. When the Naval War College was established on the island in 1884 the building that had been used as the headquarters of the training system was transferred to the college, although space in it was retained for the training service. The latter was housed in ships and on the island in the rigging loft and in tents, and in the War College building. In 1889 the Naval War College was consolidated with the Torpedo Station on Goat Island.

As a part of the reorganization of the Navy Department effected by General Order No. 372 of June 25, 1889, the naval apprentice system was transferred to the supervision of the Bureau of Navigation where it continued to be operated along the same lines. Another training station for apprentices was established on the Pacific coast on Yerba Buena Island, in San Francisco Bay, on March 25, 1899. By the close of the Spanish-American War the naval apprentice system had successfully reduced the number of foreign seamen in the Navy to a small percentage.

For other records relating to apprentices, see entries 28 and 29 in the Preliminary Inventory of the Records of the Bureau of Yards and Docks and entry 93 in the Checklist of the Naval Records Collection.

CERTIFICATES OF CONSENT FOR MINORS TO ENTER THE NAVAL SERVICE ("CERTIFICATES NO. 1"). 1838-40. 1 vol. 2 in.   241

These records were probably "inherited" from the Office of the Secretary, since neither the Bureau of Navigation nor the Bureau of Equipment and Recruiting were in existence at the time they were created. The forms, entitled "Certificate by an Absent Parent or Guardian," were signed by the parents or guardians of underage boys to give consent for the boys to enter the Navy. The person signing also certified to the date of the boy's birth and to the fact of parenthood or guardianship. Arranged in general chronologically by year.

CERTIFICATES OF CONSENT TO ENLISTMENTS OF NAVAL APPRENTICES ("ENLISTMENTS OF NAVAL APPRENTICES"). Jan. 3-Aug. 7, 1867. 1 vol. 2 in. 242

This is the same type of record as that described in entry 241 except that the form had been changed to add an "Oath of Allegiance by Naval Apprentice," executed before the recruiting officer, and a "Descriptive List" of physical data for each apprentice. Arranged chronologically.

RECORDS RELATING TO ENLISTMENT OF UNDERAGE MEN AS APPRENTICES ("APPRENTICE PAPERS"). July 1864-Sept. 1889. 11 ft. 243

Consist mainly of printed forms signed by parents or guardians, accompanied up to 1869 by testimonials and other letters received concerning or in behalf of the apprentices. The series also includes some miscellaneous letters and papers among which are copies of letters from the Chief of the Bureau of Equipment and Recruiting to navy yards relating to the administration of the apprentice program. Arranged alphabetically by initial two letters of apprentice's name.

WEEKLY REPORTS OF "BOYS" AND APPRENTICES RECEIVED ON BOARD NAVAL VESSELS. June 26, 1875-Dec. 31, 1894. 34 vols. 5 ft. 244

These weekly reports, on printed forms, were begun by the Bureau of Equipment and Recruiting as "Weekly Report of Boys" and the first 20 volumes are so labeled. After December 31, 1888, the title of the form was changed to "Weekly Report of Apprentices" and volumes 21-34 are labeled "Bureau of Navigation." The reports were submitted by naval vessels and show the number of boys or apprentices received from all sources, and discharges, desertions, deaths, number on board, and status. The reports are arranged chronologically.

RECORD OF NAVAL APPRENTICES ("RECORD OF BOYS," "RECORD OF APPRENTICES"). Feb. 1880-Dec. 1897. 3 vols. 4 in. 245

These volumes are a combined record of service and an index to an enlistment book that has not been found. The following information is given: place and date of enlistment, name of vessel to which assigned, reference to enlistment book, and date of expiration of service. The names are entered under the year, thereunder alphabetically by first letter of name, and thereunder by date of enlistment.

JOURNAL OF ENLISTMENTS OF NAVAL APPRENTICES ON THE RECEIVING SHIP ALLEGHANY. Aug. 28, 1865-Mar. 10, 1868. 1 vol. 1 in. 246

Contains printed forms entitled "Transcript List" (giving enlistment and service data) and "Descriptive List" (giving personal data) relating to apprentices received on board the ship. Arranged chronologically.

GENERAL RECORD OF NAVAL APPRENTICES RECEIVED ON BOARD THE APPRENTICE
    SHIP PORTSMOUTH. June 1867-July 1868. 1 vol. 1 in.   247

    This volume contains forms showing, on the left-hand page, name of the apprentice, personal data, enlistment data, and date he was received on board; and on the right-hand page, his general standing, his transfers to and returns from cruisers, and date of his discharge. Arranged by number of apprentice. The volume is indexed alphabetically by initial letter of apprentice's name.

DESCRIPTIVE MUSTER ROLL OF THE APPRENTICE SHIP SABINE. July 1864-
    Apr. 1868. 1 vol. 1 in.   248

    This volume contains forms showing number, name, and rating of each apprentice; date, place, and term of enlistment; name of place or vessel from which he was received; date he was received on board; place of birth; a personal description; information on the disposition of the apprentice, i.e., transferred, discharged, or died; and remarks. Arranged chronologically by date apprentice was received on board.

RETURNS OF APPRENTICES ENLISTED FOR DUTY ABOARD THE SABINE. July 18,
    1864-June 22, 1868. 1 vol. 3/4 in.   249

    This volume contains printed forms that were submitted for apprentices who had been enlisted at Boston, Mass., and New London, Conn. Names of recruits and enlistment data, together with a personal description of each boy, are given. The forms are arranged in two sections according to the place of enlistment and thereunder chronologically by date of enlistment.

GENERAL RECORD OF NAVAL APPRENTICES RECEIVED ON BOARD THE APPRENTICE
    SHIP SABINE. July 1864-Aug. 1865. 1 vol. 1 in.   250

    This volume contains the same type of information, and on the same form, as that described in entry 247.

RECORDS RELATING TO APPRENTICE TRAINING METHODS USED ABOARD THE SABINE
    ("NAVAL APPRENTICE FORMS"). Nov. 19-Dec. 8, 1864. 1 vol. 2 in.
   251

    Consist of letters, reports, and fair copies of forms, including schedules of exercises and documents concerning individual apprentices. The records relate to the methods and routines of training used. Arranged in general chronologically.

KEYS TO ENLISTMENT RETURNS OF BOYS. 1864-69; 1875-85. 2 vols. 4 in.
   252

    These volumes contain copies of a form, "Key to Enlistment of Boys," that shows the name of the boy, name of rendezvous or vessel, date of enlistment, page number, names of persons giving consent, and remarks. The page references are to volumes in the series described in entry 219. Arranged alphabetically by initial letter of boy's name.

REGISTER OF ENLISTMENTS OF NAVAL APPRENTICES. July 1864-Oct. 1875.
   1 vol. 2 in.   253

The series covers enlistments aboard the apprentice ships Sabine, Portsmouth, and Saratoga. On one page are listed "The facts and other circumstances of their enlistment" and on the opposite page "Their history subsequent to enlistment prior to their discharge." Arranged chronologically by date boy was received on board. Indexed alphabetically by name. For an earlier series of returns of boys entered as naval apprentices, July 1837-August 1842, see entry 93 of the Checklist of the Naval Records Collection.

OTHER GENERAL RECORDS, 1861-1945

ANNUAL REPORTS FOR THE FISCAL YEARS 1897-98 THROUGH 1903-4. 4 vols.
   5 in.   254

Annual reports of the Chief of the Bureau of Navigation to the Secretary of the Navy, including reports to the Chief from activities under his jurisdiction. The volumes are arranged in part chronologically; the reports within each volume are unarranged.

COPIES OF NAVAL MILITIA BILLS. ca. 1909-10. 1 vol. 3/4 in.   255

These are printed extracts of bills, together with emendations, affecting the Naval Militia. Arranged by section of the bill. An index in the front of the volume briefs the different sections but does not refer to page numbers as the volume is unpaged.

SUMMARIES OF SERVICE OF NAVAL VESSELS IN THE MEXICAN WAR. Feb. 28,
   1879-Oct. 7, 1884. 1/4 in.   256

This series consists of memorandums to the Commissioner of Pensions and the Chief of the Bureau of Navigation; a report of the Fourth Auditor of the Treasury forwarded to the Chief of the Bureau relating to the service of certain U. S. ships in the Mexican War; and a list of such ships, showing inclusive periods of service, together with several other enclosures. Some pages are missing. Arranged in the order described. For a volume containing similar information see entry 96.

LIST OF CAPTORS AND OF PRIZE VESSELS TAKEN DURING THE CIVIL WAR ("CAPTORS"). n.d. 1 vol. 1/8 in.   257

This volume shows the names of the capturing vessel and the captured vessel, the type of the captured vessel's cargo, and other data about it. Arranged in general alphabetically by name of capturing vessel.

LISTS OF DECREES IN PRIZE CASES RESULTING FROM THE CIVIL WAR. n.d.
   1 vol. 1/4 in.   258

This volume lists the vessels captured as prizes by the "North" during the Civil War, amounts of money involved or realized, and other details such as names of vessels or persons to share in proceeds of the sales. Arranged by city, as "Boston Cases," with entries thereunder by name of vessel.

PLANS AND PHOTOGRAPHS OF NAVAL OPERATING BASE AT LEYTE GULF, PHILIPPINE
ISLANDS. Oct. 1944-Sept. 1945. 1 vol. 5 in. 258-A
A bound portfolio containing historical and general information about
the area and the construction of various facilities of the base. The
volume contains charts, plans for construction, maps of the locality,
and many pictures illustrating the progress of the construction and the
use of the completed facilities.

Applications and Registers, 1861-1915

REGISTERS OF EMPLOYEES. ca. 1861-89. 3 vols. 8 in. 259
Consist of: (1) a volume, ca. 1861-62, containing data on employees,
arranged in sections by yard, station, Navy Department, advertising, and
miscellaneous and thereunder by name of employee; (2) a volume labeled
"Navy Yard and Navy Department," ca. 1875-82, arranged in the same manner; and (3) a volume labeled "Miscellaneous," 1862-89, containing a
list of employees that shows the serial number, name, type of position,
and sponsor of each, arranged chronologically by date of beginning employment. The volumes are indexed alphabetically by name of employee.

RECORD OF APPLICATIONS AND APPOINTMENTS AT NAVY YARDS ("NAVY YARDS AND
NAVY DEPARTMENT"). Nov. 1882-June 1886. 1 vol. 2 in. 260
This volume contains entries giving the following information: date
of application or appointment, serial number, name of applicant or appointee, position, and any special notation as to patron. Arranged by
yard and thereunder chronologically. The volume is indexed alphabetically by name of applicant or appointee.

PRESS COPIES OF LETTERS SENT TO APPLICANTS FOR EMPLOYMENT IN THE NAVY
DEPARTMENT. Sept. 21, 1885-Aug. 17, 1886. 1 vol. 1 in. 261
These are copies of form letters sent by the Office of the Secretary
of the Navy to applicants for all types of positions in Washington and
at such field establishments as navy yards. Arranged chronologically.
The volume is indexed in general alphabetically by name of applicant.

LIST OF MASTER WORKMEN, CLERKS, AND WRITERS AT NAVY YARDS. 1885-86.
5 in. 262
These forms, submitted monthly to the Secretary of the Navy, show the
name of employee, his rating, the department to which he was assigned,
the date of his appointment, the authority for his appointment, and the
per-diem pay. Arranged in folded groups of one or more reports, but
with no consistent arrangement thereunder.

OFFERS OF AND APPLICATIONS FOR NAVAL SERVICE. Feb.-Dec. 1898. 1 ft.
263
This series consists mainly of letters received from applicants for
positions or from persons making inquiries, together with press copies
of letters sent in reply, usually with an attached slip indicating a

cross-reference to one of several series of press copies of letters sent by the Bureau (see various series described in entries 2-71). The series includes some requests from officers for active sea duty. Most of the letters received were apparently prompted by the probability of war with Spain. Arranged alphabetically by name of correspondent.

RECORD OF NOMINATIONS OF PAYMASTERS CLERKS. 1898-1904. 1 vol.   263-A

This volume contains entries giving name of clerk, jacket and file numbers of correspondence concerning appointment, date of appointment, home address, name of person who made the nomination, and date of revocation or expiration of appointment. Arranged chronologically. The volume is indexed alphabetically by name of clerk.

REGISTER OF PAYMASTERS CLERKS. 1898. 1 vol. 2 in.   263-B

This volume contains entries giving the following information for paymasters clerks attached to ships, auxiliary vessels, navy yards, or stations: date of oath, name of appointee, and place from which appointed. Arranged alphabetically by name of ship or other activity. The volume is "treble-indexed" by name of vessel, name of paymaster, and name of paymasters clerk.

REGISTER OF PAYMASTERS CLERKS. 1898-1915. 1 vol. 4 in.   263-C

Entries in the volume show name of clerk, name and rank of pay officer, duty, home address, date of appointment, and date of return home. Some of the entries also include such information as clerk's birth date, qualifications, and conduct. The volume contains relatively few entries. After 1915 a card system was used for this type of information.

Records Showing Complements of Ships and Shore Units, 1891-1913

FORMS SHOWING COMPLEMENTS OF NAVAL VESSELS. 1891-93; 1895-1901.
2 vols. 6 in.   264

The volumes contain copies of Bureau of Navigation unnumbered form "Complement of U.S.S. _____," showing the total complement under various classes and ratings on a vessel and the grand total for that vessel. The earliest volume also contains printed plans and pictures of vessels. Each volume is arranged alphabetically by name of ship.

FORMS SHOWING COMPLEMENTS OF DESTROYERS, TORPEDO BOATS, SHORE STATIONS, AND NAVAL MILITIA VESSELS. 1897-1904. 1 vol. 3 in.   265

These forms are the same type as those described in entry 264 and are arranged in the same manner.

FORMS SHOWING COMPLEMENTS OF VESSELS AND SHORE ESTABLISHMENTS. 1906-13.
1 vol. 4 in.   266

These are forms of the Bureau of Navigation entitled "Complement of the U.S.S. _____," giving the number of officers and men under various ratings, ratings by branch or group, total complement, notations, and recapitulation figures. Lists for a given ship or shore unit are usually arranged in reverse chronological order. The volume is indexed by classification, as vessel, yard, station, or other shore unit, and thereunder alphabetically by name of such unit.

Watch, Quarter, and Station Bill Books, 1887-1911

WATCH, QUARTER, AND STATION BILL BOOKS. 1887-1911. 87 vols. 5 ft. 267

These volumes were used on ships as manuals of regulations, organization, and complement. They show the assignment and distribution of personnel as well as the type of equipment and materials and the use to which they were put. There is some variation in the content and manner of keeping these volumes. Most of the volumes list personnel by division or other unit, show stations to which personnel were assigned, and under "bills" describe just how each man was to proceed under given conditions. A "Fire Bill," for example, shows each man's station and duties in the event of fire. The volumes also include tables showing the arms, ammunition, and provisions a given boat is to carry and how it is to employ and distribute them. A few volumes cover as late a period as 1917-20. Volumes are arranged alphabetically by name of vessel, Abalone-Yorktown; within volumes the arrangement varies. At the end of the series are two undated volumes not identifiable with any vessel. A few volumes are indexed.

Photographic Records

For other photographic records described in this inventory, see especially entries 176, 177, and 380.

MISCELLANEOUS PHOTOGRAPHS. n.d. 2 ft. 268

Photographs, probably taken during the World War I period, of officers and men, vessels, shore units, buildings, and other Navy facilities. The photographs document training activities and so are related to the activities of the Sixth (or Morale) Division or the Training Division, records of which are described elsewhere in this inventory. The photographs vary widely in size, some rolled photographs being several feet in length. Unarranged.

GLASS PLATE NEGATIVES. 1917-26. 1 ft. 268-A

Approximately 300 negatives used by the Navy Recruiting Bureau in public relations activities.

GLASS LANTERN SLIDES. ca. 1925. 4 in. 268-B

Approximately 100 black-and-white and colored slides used by the Navy Recruiting Bureau in an effort to make a career in the Navy attractive.

PHOTOGRAPHS OF NAVY PERSONNEL. 1917-19. 7 ft. 268-C

Approximately 4,000 photographs, either glass plate negatives or prints, of Navy personnel who either died in World War I or received awards for wartime service. These photographs were made or assembled by the Bureau of Navigation.

MOTION PICTURES OF NAVY ACTIVITIES DURING AND AFTER WORLD WAR I. n.d. 102 reels. 269

These films were produced either by the Navy or by commercial firms for Navy recruiting purposes. There are 101 reels of positive film and 1 reel of negative film (35 mm.), some unedited or only roughly edited. Scenes are shown of practically all Navy activities on both land and sea, such as those of battleships, destroyers, seaplanes, the U. S. Fleet in foreign waters, and training camps. Arranged by receipt-invoice number, thereunder by a numeric-subject system. There is an index on 3" x 5" cards, by subject and title.

Cartographic Records

MAPS RELATING TO THE SPANISH-AMERICAN WAR. 1898. 4 items. 269-A

Manuscript maps illustrating naval activities of the Spanish-American War. Three maps show the positions and the courses sailed by the American and Spanish ships off Santiago, Cuba, on July 3, 1898, and a map of the Atlantic Ocean shows the track of Admiral Ceveras' squadron from Spain to Cuba, April 1 to July 3, 1898.

ADMINISTRATIVE MAPS. 1919 and 1935. 2 items. 269-B

Published base maps of the United States, overprinted to show the U. S. naval recruiting organization districts and divisions together with district and division headquarters.

MAP RECORDS OF THE NAVAL WAR COLLEGE. 1905-32. 9 items. 269-C

Photoprocessed maps consisting of a general map of northeastern Colombia, 1905; strategic charts of the world, 1913, the Atlantic and Pacific Oceans, 1912, and the Pacific Ocean, 1929, showing distances; and a series of bound maps with related tabular data from economic and strategic studies of foreign trade, trade areas, shipping, the vulnerability of the principal maritime nations, and the like, 1932.

RECORDS OF THE OFFICE OF DETAIL, 1865-90

An Office of Detail was established in the Office of the Secretary of the Navy in 1861 to handle the detailing of officers. On April 28, 1865, it was placed under the Chief of the Bureau of Navigation and that Bureau was known as the Bureau of Navigation and Office of Detail. Thereafter the Bureau Chief signed routine orders to naval officers "By direction of the Secretary of the Navy;" and on June 26, 1869, he was given authority to issue orders to staff officers as well as line officers. Control over the movements of naval vessels was assigned to the Bureau by an order of the Secretary dated November 28, 1881, that directed commandants of navy yards, commanders of squadrons, and commanding officers of ships to send all reports, letters, and telegrams relating to the movements of ships to the Bureau of Navigation and Office of Detail. The Chief of that Bureau was to keep records of their positions and destinations and to prepare orders and instructions for the signature of the Secretary. A change in the administration of the Navy Department, however, resulted in the return to the Secretary's Office of the functions of detailing officers and controlling the movements of ships. General Order No. 309 of October 15, 1883, directed that "All communications to the Navy Department from officers of the Navy, excepting only such as relate strictly to the specific duties of the various Bureaus, as defined in General Order No. 293, dated March 30, 1882, will be addressed to the Secretary of the Navy." A further order of October 1, 1884, returned the Office of Detail to the Secretary's Office. A new Secretary, however, restored it to the Bureau of Navigation on May 22, 1885, where it continued to function until the entire Navy Department was reorganized in accordance with General Order No. 372 of June 25, 1889. At that time the Office was absorbed by the Bureau and in its stead a Division of Officers and Fleet was set up (see p. 107).

Some series of records begun by the Office of Detail but continued for a longer period of time by the Division of Officers and Fleet are described as a part of the Division's records. In other series the reverse is true, so that there is some overlapping in dates between the series of records attributed to the Office and those attributed to the Division.

Separate correspondence volumes were maintained for the Office of Detail after it was attached to the Bureau of Navigation in May 1865. Most of the letters were addressed to officers and were signed by the Chief of the Bureau by direction of the Secretary. Some of the press copies were retained by the Office but most of them are a part of the records of the Secretary's Office, described in the Preliminary Checklist of the General Records of the Department of the Navy. Incoming letters were retained by the Office of Detail and bound in volumes according to class of correspondent for the years 1865-86. Most of the letters received series terminate at the end of December 1886; there are, however, registers containing brief abstracts of letters for the years 1887-90 (see entry 107). In January 1887 there was begun the system of filing incoming letters folded and in document containers. Until July 1889 the letters bear the stamp of the Office of Detail; after that date they bear the stamp of the Division of Officers and Fleet (see entries 392-394). For other records relating to officers, see the table of contents.

FAIR COPIES OF MISCELLANEOUS LETTERS SENT. May 11, 1865-Nov. 3, 1884; Nov. 1-16, 1889. 17 vols. 4 ft. 270
These letters and telegrams relate to or order the assignment, trans-

fer, leave, and discharge of officers. They informed the bureaus concerned of such changes in duty and reported them to the Fourth Auditor of the Treasury Department; furnished service records to outside inquirers; and provided general information to a variety of correspondents. Arranged chronologically. The volumes are indexed alphabetically by initial letter of officer's name. The registers of the Bureau's general correspondence described in entry 103 may be helpful as a guide to these letters.

PRESS COPIES OF LETTERS SENT. Dec. 5, 1887-Jan. 15, 1890. 2 vols. 2 in. 271

Mainly copies of letters, but including some copies of telegrams, that were signed by the Chief of the Bureau of Navigation and addressed to other bureaus of the Navy Department and to the general public. They relate to the movements of vessels, the whereabouts of officers, administrative matters, and other general subjects. Arranged chronologically. The volumes are indexed alphabetically by initial letter of name, naval unit or bureau, or other Government department. The registers of the Bureau's general correspondence described in entry 103 may be helpful as a guide to these letters.

LETTERS RECEIVED FROM REAR ADMIRALS, ADMIRALS, COMMODORES, CAPTAINS, AND COMMANDERS. May 13, 1865-Oct. 27, 1884; Jan. 1, 1885-Dec. 31, 1886. 52 vols. 13 ft. 272

Include letters, form letters, reports, copies of orders, and telegrams. Through 1869 there are two numbered volumes for each year; after that, one or more unnumbered volumes per year. This series illustrates the shifting of authority that occurred in the detailing of officers. From May 13, 1865-February 12, 1882, letters are addressed to the Bureau of Navigation and Office of Detail; from February 13, 1882-March 1, 1885, the received stamp of the Office of Detail alone appears; and from March 2-December 31, 1886, the correspondence is stamped with the stamp of the Detail Division, Secretary's Office. Arranged in general chronologically. The volumes are indexed alphabetically by initial letter of officer's name. For registers that serve as a guide to the subject matter of the letters, see entry 277.

LETTERS RECEIVED FROM OFFICERS COMMANDING FLEETS, NAVAL FORCES ON STATION, AND SQUADRONS ("SQUADRONS"). May 13, 1865-Dec. 20, 1872. 6 vols. 1 ft. 273

Include letters, despatches, telegrams, and reports, with such types of enclosures as lists of officers and copies of orders. Arranged by squadron and fleet and thereunder chronologically. The volumes are indexed by squadron or fleet. For registers, see entry 277.

LETTERS RECEIVED FROM COMMANDANTS OF NAVY YARDS AND STATIONS, THE NAVAL ACADEMY, AND THE NAVAL OBSERVATORY ("NAVY YARDS," "COMMANDANTS"). May 23, 1865-Nov. 30, 1869; Jan. 3, 1872-Dec. 31, 1873; Jan. 12, 1885-Dec. 31, 1886. 16 vols. 3 ft. 274

This series includes letters, form letters, telegrams, reports, lists of officers and vessels, and acknowledgments of orders. One volume consists of letters from the commandants of the Naval Academy and the Naval Observatory. Letters in the 1885-86 group are addressed to the Secretary of the Navy and bear the received stamp of the Detail Division. Arranged by yard, station, or establishment and thereunder chronologically. The volumes are indexed by yard, station, or establishment and thereunder in general alphabetically by name of officer. For registers, see entry 277.

LETTERS RECEIVED FROM LIEUTENANT COMMANDERS AND OTHER OFFICERS ("OFFICERS LETTERS"). May 8, 1865-Dec. 31, 1886. 240 vols. 54 ft. 275

Include letters, form letters, telegrams, and cablegrams received from officers of the rank of lieutenant commander and below. Mainly they report arrival in the United States, change of address, receipt of or compliance with orders, and state of health if officer was recuperating; and request detailing, change of duty, leave, or discharge. The volumes are numbered through October 1866 and thereafter unnumbered. Arranged chronologically. The volumes are indexed alphabetically by initial letter of officer's name. For registers, see entry 277.

MISCELLANEOUS LETTERS RECEIVED CONCERNING ROUTINE PERSONNEL MATTERS ("MISCELLANEOUS LETTERS"). Mar. 20, 1865-Dec. 29, 1869; July 2, 1885-Dec. 31, 1886. 11 vols. 2 ft. 276

Letters and telegrams from both Government and non-Government sources, together with a few cablegrams and a variety of enclosures. The earlier volumes relate to more or less routine personnel matters such as pay, leave, reinstatement, discharges, whereabouts, and service records of men in or formerly in the naval service. The later volumes contain somewhat more varied inquiries, reflecting the expansion of personnel functions that had taken place. Arranged chronologically. The volumes are indexed by initial letter of name of correspondent. For registers, see entry 277.

REGISTERS OF LETTERS RECEIVED BY THE OFFICE OF DETAIL ("KEY TO LETTERS RECEIVED"). May 1865-Dec. 1890. 20 vols. 7 ft. 277

This series consists of 16 numbered volumes, 1865-87; volumes "B" and "C," 1888; an unnumbered volume, 1889; and another unnumbered volume, 1889-90, apparently begun by the Division of Officers and Fleet in 1889 when it succeeded the Office of Detail. Each volume has two sections: (1) an alphabetical section in which daily entries were made by name of correspondent; and (2) a section in which entries were made by squadron, flotilla, navy yard, bureau and special office of the Navy Department, or Government department and division thereof, and thereunder chronologically. The letters received that are registered in these volumes are described in entries 272-276 and 392. A preliminary register, apparently maintained in the Office of Detail, is described in entry 83 of the Checklist of the Naval Records Collection.

REPORT OF NAVAL CADETS ON SHIPS. Dec. 31, 1884-Dec. 31, 1890. 1 vol.
2 in. 278

This volume, apparently kept originally in the Office of the Secretary of the Navy, consists of forms entitled "Report of Naval Cadets attached to the U.S.S. _____, _____ Rate, _____ Station for quarter ending _____, 188_" that were signed by the commanding officer of the vessel. The form, submitted in conformity with Navy Regulation No. 37, furnished data to the Academic Board of the Naval Academy for use in forming an estimate of the aptitude of naval cadets for the naval service. Each form is stamped "Office of Detail," and contains the names of cadets and the ratings given them on performance of duty under various categories. The volume may be a part of the records of the Office of Detail only by inheritance from the Office of the Secretary. Arranged alphabetically by name of vessel and thereunder chronologically by quarter.

RECORDS OF THE BUREAU OF EQUIPMENT AND RECRUITING, 1856-1928

Among the bureaus created in the reorganization authorized by an act of Congress of July 5, 1862, was the Bureau of Equipment and Recruiting. From the former Bureau of Construction, Equipment, and Repair it took over certain duties relating to material, but it became mainly occupied with handling the enlisted personnel of the Navy. In addition to its supervision of the equipment of officers and recruiting officers, the Bureau in 1875 acquired the direction of the apprentice training system that was reestablished at that time.

When the Navy Department was reorganized in 1889 the Bureau of Navigation was assigned functions relating to personnel and the fleet. As a result, the handling of enlisted personnel, recruiting, and the apprentice system was transferred from the Bureau of Equipment and Recruiting to the Bureau of Navigation. In 1891 the name of the Bureau was changed to the Bureau of Equipment, and in 1910 it was discontinued although not formally abolished until June 30, 1914.

In conformity with the change in method of keeping correspondence that was made throughout the Navy Department in 1885, it is assumed that the Bureau changed from the use of bound volumes to the use of the folded file system. If so, letters received for the years 1886-89 have been lost, with the exception of a few 1889 letters included in the miscellaneous letters described in entry 351. It is believed that many of these missing letters have become a part of enlisted personnel jackets, compilation of which began in 1885. Correspondence of the Bureau of Equipment, 1899-1910, is a part of the records in Record Group 19, Records of the Bureau of Ships.

CORRESPONDENCE, 1862-92

Letters Sent, 1862-89

LETTERS SENT ("RECORD OF LETTERS SENT"). Mar. 2, 1885-Dec. 31, 1889.
   14 vols. 3 ft.   279
   Consist of fair and typewritten copies of letters and telegrams sent to all classes of correspondents, apparently continuing a number of the earlier series of letters sent that are described below. The letters relate mainly to the same subjects as these separate series except for letters dated after June 1889 when the Bureau of Equipment and Recruiting lost its personnel functions and became the Bureau of Equipment. The letters are arranged chronologically, several volumes labeled "A," "B," or "C," as the case might be, for 1 year. For separate indexes, see entries 352 and 356.

FAIR COPIES OF LETTERS SENT TO THE SECRETARY OF THE NAVY. Oct. 4, 1862-
   Mar. 1, 1870; Jan. 17, 1882-Dec. 28, 1883. 2 vols. 5 in.   280
   Relate to appropriations estimates, annual reports, proposed legislation affecting the Navy Department, suggestions regarding policy and projected work of the Bureau, and other high-level administrative and policy matters that would normally be brought to the attention of the Secretary of the Navy. Arranged chronologically. Part of volume 1 is indexed chronologically. For registers, see entry 351. For press copies of letters sent to the Secretary, see entry 281.

PRESS COPIES OF LETTERS SENT TO THE SECRETARY OF THE NAVY. Oct. 4, 1862-
   Feb. 28, 1885. 5 vols. 7 in.   281
   These duplicate the fair copies described in entry 280 and include, in addition, copies of letters that are missing from that series. Arranged chronologically. Volume 1 contains a chronological list of the letters; volumes 2 and 3 are not indexed; and volumes 4 and 5 are indexed alphabetically by name and subject. For registers, see entry 351.

FAIR COPIES OF LETTERS SENT TO THE FOURTH AUDITOR OF THE TREASURY DE-
   PARTMENT. Jan. 3, 1865-Sept. 29, 1882; Jan. 3, 1882-Dec. 27, 1883.
   3 vols. 8 in.   282
   The Fourth Auditor headed a bureau in the Treasury Department handling Navy and Marine accounts and figured importantly in deciding pension and bounty claims of Navy men. Many of these letters concern the adjustment of accounts of Navy men, transmit accounts of paymasters, request information from records, or furnish information required by the Fourth Auditor, usually concerning naval service records. Arranged chronologically. For registers, see entry 351. For press copies of letters sent to the Fourth Auditor, see entry 283. A series containing letters received from the Fourth Auditor is described in entry 331.

PRESS COPIES OF LETTERS SENT TO THE FOURTH AUDITOR OF THE TREASURY DE-
   PARTMENT. Jan. 3, 1865-Feb. 28, 1885. 11 vols. 1 ft.   283
   These letters, including filled-in form letters, are duplicated in

part by the fair copies described in entry 282. Arranged chronologically. Volume 1 contains a list of the letters in the order of their arrangement; volumes 2-8 are not indexed; and volumes 9-11 are indexed in part alphabetically by name. For registers, see entry 351.

PRESS COPIES OF LETTERS SENT TO THE COMMISSIONER OF PENSIONS. Apr. 3, 1871-Feb. 27, 1885. 5 vols. 6 in.   284

Many of these are form letters transmitting "descriptive lists" of applicants for pensions, applications for pensions, histories of service, and legal documents in support of pension claims. The letters duplicate part of the fair copies described in entry 285. Arranged chronologically. The volumes are indexed alphabetically by name of applicant for pension. For registers, see entry 351.

FAIR COPIES OF LETTERS SENT TO THE COMMISSIONER OF PENSIONS. Jan. 8, 1882-Dec. 29, 1883. 1 vol. 2 in.   285

This unlabeled volume contains copies of letters that document steps in the procurement of pensions for Navy men who had made application. They are duplicated in part by the press copies of letters described in entry 284. Arranged chronologically. For registers, see entry 351.

FAIR COPIES OF LETTERS SENT TO THE SUPERINTENDENT OF THE NAVAL ACADEMY. Sept. 29, 1865-May 31, 1869. 1 vol. 2 in.   286

This volume, designated as "No. 1," contains copies of letters sent, together with some orders, that relate to the supply of certain stores and equipment under the jurisdiction of the Bureau of Equipment and Recruiting at this time, housekeeping and administrative matters, discharges and transfers of apprentices and enlisted men, and other personnel matters. Arranged chronologically. For registers, see entry 351. These letters are duplicated in part by the press copies described in entry 287.

PRESS COPIES OF LETTERS SENT TO THE SUPERINTENDENT OF THE NAVAL ACADEMY. Sept. 29, 1865-Dec. 31, 1883. 3 vols. 4 in.   287

This series, including copies of form letters and telegrams, relates mainly to the supply of certain stores and equipment under jurisdiction of the Bureau at this time; to personnel, particularly discharges and transfers of enlisted men and apprentices and the furnishing of men for assignment to such practice, training, and other Navy vessels as were under cognizance of the Academy; and to routine housekeeping matters. Arranged chronologically. For registers, see entry 351. For fair copies of letters sent to the Academy for part of this period, see entry 286.

LETTERS SENT TO MANUFACTURERS OF CHINA, GLASS, AND PLATED WARE ("C. G. & P. WARE"). June 16, 1869-Dec. 26, 1882. 4 vols. 5 in.   288

Press copies of letters, including form letters, and telegrams from the Chief of the Bureau to manufacturers and dealers in china, glass, and plated ware. Most of the letters relate to the ordering of and payment for such articles, which were furnished usually to commanders of naval vessels; some also transmit badges for engraving. Arranged chronologically. For registers, see entry 351.

FAIR COPIES OF MISCELLANEOUS LETTERS SENT. Sept. 3, 1862-Oct. 10, 1870; Jan. 3, 1882-Oct. 25, 1883. 6 vols. 1 ft. 289

These letters, sent by the Bureau to persons outside the Government, were for the most part in answer to inquiries about Navy enlisted men though some letters pertaining to other matters are included. This is correspondence that is not readily assignable to any other series. Arranged chronologically. Four of the volumes are indexed alphabetically by name of addressee. For registers, see entry 351. These letters are duplicated, insofar as dates coincide, by the press copies described in entry 290.

PRESS COPIES OF MISCELLANEOUS LETTERS SENT. Sept. 3, 1862-Feb. 28, 1885. 82 vols. 9 ft. 290

These letters duplicate, insofar as dates coincide, the fair copies described in entry 289. Arranged chronologically. Most of the volumes are indexed alphabetically by name of person or business firm, by official title or office held, or by subject. For registers, see entry 351.

Letters Sent to Commanders of Squadrons and Naval Forces, 1865-83

FAIR COPIES OF LETTERS SENT TO COMMANDERS OF SQUADRONS AND NAVAL FORCES ON STATION ("COMMANDERS OF SQUADRONS"). Jan. 10, 1865-June 24, 1871; Jan. 3, 1882-Dec. 27, 1883. 2 vols. 5 in. 291

Relate to enlisted personnel and to the supplying of vessels with such equipment and stores as were under the Bureau's cognizance. The letters relating to enlisted personnel include general instructions and circulars and concern transfers, discharges, enlistments, details, the submission and correction of personnel and service records, and bounty payments (to June 30, 1865). Many of the letters relating to supplies concern the coaling and equipment of ships and the furnishing of them with supplies and stores; a few relate to Bureau contracts for supplies and stores. The earlier volume is arranged by squadron or station and thereunder chronologically; the later volume is arranged chronologically. The earlier volume is indexed in part alphabetically by name. For registers, see entry 351. The press copies of letters sent (described in entries 292-299 and 329) are similar in subject matter, are for the same general period, and in some cases duplicate the fair copies in this series.

PRESS COPIES OF LETTERS SENT TO COMMANDERS OF SQUADRONS AND NAVAL FORCES ON STATION ("SQUADRONS"). Jan. 7-Dec. 11, 1873; Jan. 3, 1881-Dec. 27, 1883. 3 vols. 4 in. 292

Copies of letters that are similar in subject matter to the fair copies described in entry 291 and, where dates coincide, are duplicates of them. In the earliest volume the letters are arranged by squadron and thereunder chronologically; in the two succeeding volumes the letters are arranged chronologically. The earliest volume has an index preceding the letters sent to each squadron. For registers, see entry 351. For other press copies of letters sent to squadrons and naval forces on station, see entries 293-299 and entry 329.

LETTERS SENT TO THE COMMANDER OF THE NAVAL FORCE ON ASIATIC STATION. Aug. 11, 1865-Nov. 17, 1881. 1 vol. 1 in. 293
These press copies are for the same general period and are similar in subject matter to the fair copies described in entries 291 and 292. Arranged chronologically. For registers, see entry 351.

LETTERS SENT TO THE COMMANDER OF THE NORTH ATLANTIC SQUADRON. Jan. 10, 1865-Dec. 10, 1881. 3 vols. 4 in. 294
Press copies of letters addressed to the Commander of the North Atlantic Squadron and the North Atlantic Fleet and to the Commander in Chief, U. S. Naval Force on North Atlantic Station. Arranged chronologically. For registers, see entry 351. These letters are for the same general period and are similar in subject matter to those described in entries 291 and 292.

LETTERS SENT TO THE COMMANDER OF THE NAVAL FORCE ON NORTH PACIFIC STATION. Feb. 9, 1874-Dec. 1, 1881. 1 vol. 1 in. 295
These press copies of letters are for the same general period and are similar in subject matter to those described in entries 291 and 292. Arranged chronologically. For registers, see entry 351.

LETTERS SENT TO COMMANDERS OF SQUADRONS AND OTHER UNITS IN SOUTH ATLANTIC WATERS ("S. ATLANTIC STATION"). July 18, 1875-Nov. 1, 1811. 1 vol. 1 in. 296
These press copies of letters are for the same general period and are similar in subject matter to those described in entries 291 and 292. Arranged chronologically. For registers, see entry 351.

LETTERS SENT TO THE COMMANDER OF THE NAVAL FORCE ON SOUTH PACIFIC STATION. Feb. 19, 1874-Feb. 9, 1878. 1 vol. 1 in. 297
These press copies of letters are for the same general period and are similar in subject matter to those described in entries 291 and 292. Arranged chronologically. For registers, see entry 351.

LETTERS SENT TO THE COMMANDER OF THE WEST GULF SQUADRON. Jan. 3, 1865-May 8, 1867. 1 vol. 1 in. 298
Press copies of letters addressed to the West Gulf Squadron, later known as the Gulf Squadron, that are for the same general period and are similar in subject matter to the records described in entries 291 and 292. Arranged chronologically. The volume contains a chronological list of the letters. For registers, see entry 351.

LETTERS SENT TO THE COMMANDERS OF SQUADRONS AND OTHER UNITS IN EUROPEAN
   WATERS. June 15, 1866-Nov. 18, 1881. 1 vol. 1 in.   299
   Press copies of letters for the same general period and similar in
subject matter to those described in entries 291 and 292. Arranged
chronologically. For registers, see entry 351.

Letters Sent to Commandants of Navy Yards and Stations, 1862-85

FAIR COPIES OF LETTERS SENT TO COMMANDANTS OF NAVY YARDS AND STATIONS.
   Oct. 6, 1862-Dec. 30, 1865. 2 vols. 5 in.   300
   These letters relate to enlisted personnel matters and to the fur-
nishing of such equipment and supplies as were under cognizance of the
Bureau at the time. In the volumes are sections for letters sent to
each of the following yards: Portsmouth, Boston, New York, Philadelphia,
Baltimore, Washington, Norfolk, Mare Island, and Pensacola. Arranged by
yard and thereunder chronologically. For registers, see entry 351.

PRESS COPIES OF LETTERS SENT TO COMMANDANTS OF NAVY YARDS AND STATIONS
   ("COMMANDANTS"). Oct. 6, 1862-Aug. 31, 1864. 5 vols. 8 in.   301
   These letters are for the same general period and are similar in
subject matter to those described in entry 300. Arranged chronologically. The earliest volume is indexed chronologically; the other volumes are indexed by yard and station, thereunder chronologically. For
registers, see entry 351.

PRESS COPIES OF LETTERS SENT TO THE COMMANDANT OF THE NAVAL STATION AT
   BALTIMORE. Sept. 1, 1864-Nov. 27, 1865. 1 vol. 1 in.   302
   Relate to personnel actions such as transfers and discharges; recruiting, training, and similar matters affecting enlisted personnel;
pay and service record matters; coaling and supply; equipment of vessels; and routine approvals and disapprovals. Arranged chronologically.
For registers, see entry 351.

PRESS COPIES OF LETTERS SENT TO THE COMMANDANT OF THE BOSTON NAVY YARD.
   Sept. 1, 1864-Feb. 28, 1885. 16 vols. 2 ft.   303
   Copies of letters, including filled-in form letters and telegrams,
similar in subject matter to and in some cases duplicated by the fair
copies described in entry 304. Arranged chronologically. A few volumes are indexed either chronologically or alphabetically by name or
subject. For registers, see entry 351.

FAIR COPIES OF LETTERS SENT TO THE COMMANDANT OF THE BOSTON NAVY YARD.
   Jan. 2, 1866-Dec. 31, 1883. 4 vols. 11 in.   304
   Relate to the supplying of ships with various articles through the
equipment officer at the yard, to recruiting, to the maintaining of enlistees' records, and to the training of apprentices and regular seamen.
The series also includes orders to and concerning enlisted men and letters concerning routine administration. Arranged chronologically. For

registers, see entry 351. Press copies of letters sent to the Commandant of the Boston Navy Yard are described in entry 303.

PRESS COPIES OF LETTERS SENT TO THE COMMANDANT OF THE MARE ISLAND NAVY YARD. Sept. 26, 1864-Feb. 28, 1885. 7 vols. 9 in. 305
These copies, including form letters and telegrams, duplicate part of the fair copies described in entry 306. Arranged chronologically. Of these numbered volumes only Volume 6 is indexed, alphabetically by name of person, vessel, or subject. For registers, see entry 351.

FAIR COPIES OF LETTERS SENT TO THE COMMANDANT OF THE MARE ISLAND NAVY YARD. Jan. 20, 1866-June 2, 1871; Jan. 3, 1882-Dec. 26, 1883. 2 vols. 5 in. 306
Relate to the supplying of ships with various articles through the equipment officer at the yard, to recruiting, to maintaining enlistees' service records, to personnel matters involving enlisted men (such as transfers and discharges), and to the training of apprentices and regular seamen. The series also includes orders to and concerning enlisted men and letters of routine acknowledgment and approval. Arranged chronologically. For registers, see entry 351. Press copies that duplicate some of these letters are described in entry 305.

FAIR COPIES OF LETTERS SENT TO THE COMMANDANT OF THE NAVAL STATION AT MOUND CITY, ILL. Jan. 3, 1865-July 5, 1871. 1 vol. 2 in. 307
Relate to personnel matters involving enlisted men (such as transfers and discharges), to recruiting, to maintaining and correcting service records, to the training of apprentices and regular seamen; and to the supplying of ships with various articles through equipment officers at the yards. The series also includes orders to and about enlisted men and letters of routine acknowledgment and approval. Arranged chronologically. For registers, see entry 351. For press copies of letters sent to this station, see entry 308.

PRESS COPIES OF LETTERS SENT TO THE COMMANDANT OF THE NAVAL STATION AT MOUND CITY, ILL. Jan. 3, 1865-May 19, 1873. 1 vol. 1 in. 308
Copies of letters and telegrams sent by the Chief of the Bureau. They duplicate part of the fair copies described in entry 307. Arranged chronologically. For registers, see entry 351.

PRESS COPIES OF LETTERS SENT TO THE COMMANDANT OF THE NAVAL STATION AT NEW LONDON, CONN. Jan. 2, 1880-Dec. 12, 1883. 1 vol. 1 in. 309
These copies of letters, telegrams, and form letters from the Chief of the Bureau duplicate part of the fair copies described in entry 310. Arranged chronologically. For registers, see entry 351.

FAIR COPIES OF LETTERS SENT TO THE COMMANDANT OF THE NAVAL STATION AT NEW LONDON, CONN. Feb. 23, 1882-Dec. 12, 1883. 1 vol. 3 in. 310
The records in this series are similar to those described in entry

307. Arranged chronologically. For registers, see entry 351. For press copies of letters sent to this station, see entry 309.

PRESS COPIES OF LETTERS SENT TO THE COMMANDANT OF THE NEW YORK NAVY YARD. Sept. 1, 1864-Feb. 26, 1885. 21 vols. 2 ft.   311
Copies of letters, telegrams, and form letters sent by the Chief of the Bureau. They duplicate part of the fair copies described in entry 312. Arranged chronologically. Only volumes 20 and 21 are indexed, alphabetically by name of bureau, vessel, yard, or subject. For registers, see entry 351.

FAIR COPIES OF LETTERS SENT TO THE COMMANDANT OF THE NEW YORK NAVY YARD. Jan. 2, 1866-Sept. 4, 1871; Jan. 3, 1882-Dec. 31, 1883. 3 vols. 8 in.   312
The records in this series are similar to those described in entry 306. Arranged chronologically. For registers, see entry 351. Press copies of letters sent to this yard are described in entry 311.

PRESS COPIES OF LETTERS SENT TO THE COMMANDANT OF THE NORFOLK NAVY YARD. Sept. 1, 1864-Feb. 26, 1885. 12 vols. 1 ft.   313
Copies of letters, telegrams, and form letters sent by the Chief of the Bureau. They duplicate part of the fair copies described in entry 314. Arranged chronologically. Volumes 11 and 12 are indexed alphabetically by name or subject. For registers, see entry 351.

FAIR COPIES OF LETTERS SENT TO THE COMMANDANT OF THE NORFOLK NAVY YARD. Jan. 2, 1866-Dec. 31, 1883. 3 vols. 7 in.   314
The records in this series are similar to those described in entry 306. Arranged chronologically. For registers, see entry 351. For press copies of letters sent to this yard, see entry 313.

PRESS COPIES OF LETTERS SENT TO THE COMMANDANT OF THE PENSACOLA NAVY YARD. Sept. 13, 1864-Feb. 1, 1885. 2 vols. 3 in.   315
Copies of letters, telegrams, and form letters sent by the Chief of the Bureau. They duplicate part of the fair copies described in entry 316. Arranged chronologically. For registers, see entry 351.

FAIR COPIES OF LETTERS SENT TO THE COMMANDANT OF THE PENSACOLA NAVY YARD. Jan. 2, 1866-Jan. 28, 1884. 1 vol. 2 in.   316
The records in this series are similar to those described in entry 306. Arranged chronologically. For registers, see entry 351. For press copies of letters sent to this station, see entry 315.

PRESS COPIES OF LETTERS SENT TO THE COMMANDANT OF THE PHILADELPHIA NAVY YARD. Sept. 2, 1864-Feb. 14, 1885. 15 vols. 2 ft.   317
Some of these volumes are labeled "Philadelphia," some "League Island," and a few are unlabeled. In 1875 the Philadelphia Navy Yard was moved from its original site in southeast Philadelphia to its present League

Island site, which had been acquired and developed during the 4 preceding years. One volume, for the period January 6, 1871-October 10, 1873, contains some copies of letters addressed to the Commandant of the Naval Station on League Island. The letters are similar in content to those described in entry 306. The volumes are arranged chronologically, with some overlapping and duplication of periods covered. Volumes 12 and 13 of the 13 numbered volumes are indexed alphabetically by name or subject. For registers, see entry 351.

PRESS COPIES OF LETTERS SENT TO THE COMMANDANT OF THE NAVY YARD AT PORTSMOUTH, N. H. Sept. 5, 1864-Feb. 26, 1885. 8 vols. 10 in.

318

These copies of letters and telegrams, including form letters, sent by the Chief of the Bureau duplicate part of the fair copies described in entry 319. Arranged chronologically. Volumes 7 and 8 are indexed alphabetically by name or subject. For registers, see entry 351.

FAIR COPIES OF LETTERS SENT TO THE COMMANDANT OF THE NAVY YARD AT PORTSMOUTH, N. H. Jan. 2, 1866-July 13, 1871; Jan. 4, 1882-Dec. 31, 1883. 2 vols. 4 in.
319

The records in this series are similar to those described in entry 306. Arranged chronologically. For registers, see entry 351. For press copies of letters sent to this yard, see entry 318.

PRESS COPIES OF LETTERS SENT TO THE COMMANDANT OF THE NAVY YARD AT WASHINGTON, D. C. Sept. 2, 1864-Feb. 28, 1885. 19 vols. 2 ft.

320

Copies of letters and telegrams, including form letters, sent by the Chief of the Bureau. They duplicate part of the fair copies described in entry 321. Arranged chronologically. Volumes 18 and 19 are indexed alphabetically by name or subject. For registers, see entry 351.

FAIR COPIES OF LETTERS SENT TO THE COMMANDANT OF THE NAVY YARD AT WASHINGTON, D. C. Jan. 2, 1866-Mar. 25, 1870; Jan. 3, 1882-Dec. 31, 1883. 2 vols. 5 in.
321

The records in this series are similar to those described in entry 306. Arranged chronologically. For registers, see entry 351. For press copies of letters sent to this yard, see entry 320.

Letters Sent to Other Officers, 1862-85

FAIR COPIES OF LETTERS SENT TO OFFICERS. Oct. 6, 1862-May 12, 1876; Jan. 2, 1882-Dec. 31, 1883. 12 vols. 2 ft.
322

Copies of letters and orders sent to officers commanding navy yards, stations, fleets, squadrons, flotillas, rendezvous, and vessels (including apprentice-training and receiving ships), and to recruiting officers and a few others of lower rank, such as paymasters. The correspondence relates mainly to enlisted personnel matters such as recruiting, keeping records on enlisted men, awarding medals and badges, and apprentice training. There are also letters relating to the supplying of ships with articles under cognizance of the Bureau's equipment officers stationed at navy yards and to such operating and housekeeping activities as approval of requisitions and vouchers, submission of reports, correction of existent service records, furnishing of blank forms, and soliciting information. Arranged chronologically. Most of the volumes are indexed in general alphabetically. For registers, see entry 351. For press and typewritten copies of letters sent to officers, see entry 323.

PRESS AND TYPEWRITTEN COPIES OF LETTERS SENT TO OFFICERS. Jan. 2, 1863-Feb. 28, 1885. 79 vols. 9 ft. 323
This series consists of 78 volumes of press copies and 1 volume of typewritten copies of letters sent, including filled-in form letters in the presscopy volumes. These letters, insofar as the dates coincide, are duplicated by the fair copies described in entry 322. Arranged chronologically. For registers, see entry 351. Most of the volumes are indexed alphabetically by name of officer; some of the later volumes are indexed alphabetically by name of vessel, bureau, or other entry in addition to the name.

LETTERS SENT TO NAVY AGENTS AND PAY OFFICERS. Nov. 6, 1862-Dec. 30, 1873; Jan. 3, 1882-Dec. 27, 1884. 9 vols. 1 ft. 324
This series consists of six numbered volumes labeled "Navy Agents" and three unnumbered and unlabeled volumes of letters to pay officers, all press copies. Navy agents and pay officers such as paymasters, pay inspectors, and pay directors were located at yards and other naval establishments. The letters relate to approvals and disapprovals of requisitions for stores, fuel, supplies, travel, contingent expenses and, within the limit of the function as performed by this Bureau, the equipment of vessels. Arranged chronologically. One volume labeled "Navy Agents" is indexed alphabetically by place agent was located; another volume is indexed alphabetically by name of person or vessel. For registers, see entry 351. For other press copies of letters sent to pay officers, see entries 326 and 327.

LETTERS SENT CONCERNING RECRUITING. Nov. 10, 1862-July 5, 1865. 4 vols. 5 in. 325
Press copies of letters sent by the Bureau to officers in charge of recruiting, to men seeking enlistment or reenlistment, and to persons requesting an enlisted man's whereabouts or other information from his records. Arranged chronologically. The volumes are indexed alphabetically by name of addressee. For registers, see entry 351. After July 5, 1865, recruiting letters were copied with miscellaneous letters sent (see entry 289 for fair copies and entry 290 for press copies).

LETTERS SENT TO NAVAL STOREKEEPERS. Jan. 5, 1866-Aug. 6, 1867. 1 vol. 2 in.

326

Press copies of letters sent mainly to storekeepers who were located at navy yards and stations, but in a few instances to Navy paymasters in foreign waters. Apparently these paymasters also served as storekeepers. The correspondence for the most part concerns the approval or return for correction of stores returns, invoices and vouchers, and stores inventories. Arranged chronologically. The volume is indexed in part alphabetically by name of storekeeper. For registers, see entry 351.

LETTERS SENT TO PAY OFFICERS AT NAVY YARDS. Apr. 2, 1866-Dec. 30, 1881. 38 vols. 4 ft.

327

These volumes are labeled "Purchasing Agent" or "Paymaster" and contain copies of letters and form letters (mainly approvals of requisitions) sent by the Chief of the Bureau. The letters relate to routine pay matters such as acknowledging receipt of reports, forwarding bills, and approving or directing the making of purchases. There are subseries for navy yards located at Baltimore, Boston, New York, Norfolk, Philadelphia, Portsmouth (N. H.), San Francisco, and Washington (D. C.). Within these subseries the letters are arranged chronologically. For earlier and later copies of letters sent to pay officers, see entry 324. For registers, see entry 351.

LETTERS SENT TO OFFICERS COMMANDING NAVAL VESSELS. May 12, 1876-Mar. 7, 1877. 1 vol. 2 in.

328

Fair copies of letters and orders relating to such routine matters as enlistment, training and assignment of enlisted personnel, supply and outfitting of naval vessels, pay, complements of ships, personnel actions, service records, supplies, and acknowledgments and approvals. Arranged chronologically. For registers, see entry 351.

LETTERS SENT TO THE TRAINING SQUADRONS AND THE TRAINING STATION AT NEWPORT, R. I. ("TRAINING SQUADRON"). May 21, 1881-Feb. 28, 1885. 3 vols. 4 in.

329

Press copies of letters and telegrams sent by the Chief of the Bureau to Capt. (later Commodore) S. B. Luce, commanding successively the Apprentice Training Squadron, the Training Squadron, and the Training Station at Newport. They relate to such matters as recruiting, training, assignment, transfer, and allowances of apprentices on naval vessels. The series also includes form letters approving requisitions for supplies, furniture, and stores. Arranged chronologically. Volumes 2 and 3 are indexed alphabetically by name of man, vessel, or subject. For registers, see entry 351. A corresponding series of letters received is described in entry 347.

Letters Received, 1862-92

LETTERS RECEIVED FROM THE SECRETARY OF THE NAVY. 1862-85. 5 vols. 11 in.

330

Letters, memorandums, endorsements, and form letters received by the

Bureau, many of them embodying orders to the Chief of the Bureau. They relate to Bureau functions, policy matters, and general administration; rules, regulations, and procedures; appropriations and expenditures of funds; legislation; matters affecting or requiring joint action of all bureaus of the Navy Department; and requests for reports and information. Arranged chronologically. Volume 4 is indexed alphabetically by name of person, vessel, yard, or subject. For registers, see entry 351.

LETTERS RECEIVED FROM THE FOURTH AUDITOR AND THE SECOND COMPTROLLER OF THE TREASURY DEPARTMENT. Aug. 2, 1865-Dec. 29, 1886. 17 vols. 4 ft.   <u>331</u>

Relate to such matters as transfers of men's accounts from one naval vessel to another; furnishing or requesting record-of-service information; and return of applications for claims and pensions. Arranged chronologically. Volumes 12-14 contain indexes arranged alphabetically by name of person about whom the letter was written. For registers, see entry 351. Fair copies of letters sent to the Fourth Auditor are described in entry 282.

LETTERS RECEIVED FROM THE FOURTH AUDITOR OF THE TREASURY DEPARTMENT CONCERNING BOUNTY PAYMENTS FOR SERVICE IN THE CIVIL WAR ("FOURTH AUDITOR BOUNTY"). Jan. 3-June 29, 1867. 1 vol. 3 in.   <u>332</u>

Mainly requests for information upon which bounty claims might be either granted or refused. Arranged chronologically. For registers, see entry 351.

LETTERS RECEIVED FROM THE COMMISSIONER OF PENSIONS. Dec. 26, 1882-Feb. 19, 1885. 2 vols. 3 in.   <u>333</u>

Letters, form letters, and endorsements requesting "descriptive lists" of Navy men applying for pensions. The first volume is indexed alphabetically by name of man about whom the inquiry was made. For registers, see entry 351.

LETTERS RECEIVED FROM OFFICERS. Sept. 22, 1862-Feb. 28, 1885. 194 vols. 39 ft.   <u>334</u>

Letters, endorsements, and telegrams received, mainly from officers commanding vessels, stations, and such shore establishments as the Naval Academy and the Naval Asylum, and from officers of lesser rank making routine reports and returns, as, for example, paymasters. In general the letters relate to two main functions of the Bureau, namely, certain matters of equipment and supply and almost all matters concerning enlisted personnel. Arranged chronologically. A few of the later volumes contain an "Index to officers letters" in which letters are listed and briefed by vessel, shore establishment, name, or subject and thereunder chronologically. For registers, see entry 351.

LETTERS RECEIVED FROM COMMANDANTS OF NAVY YARDS. Nov. 1, 1862-Apr. 30, 1872. 70 vols. 15 ft.   <u>335</u>

Letters received, including form letters and telegrams, that relate to the supplying of certain equipment and stores to vessels through equipment officers at the yards and to recruiting and other enlisted personnel matters. Much of the series is concerned with routine pay, reporting, administration, and housekeeping activities. Arranged chronologically. For registers, see entry 351. For later correspondence on similar subjects, arranged in series by navy yard and station, see entries 336-347.

LETTERS RECEIVED FROM THE COMMANDANT OF THE BOSTON NAVY YARD. May 2, 1872-Feb. 25, 1885. 17 vols. 4 ft. 336
These letters continue in part the series described in entry 335. Arranged chronologically. Volumes 14-16 are indexed alphabetically by name of person, vessel, or subject. For registers, see entry 351.

LETTERS RECEIVED FROM THE COMMANDANT OF THE PHILADELPHIA NAVY YARD. May 2, 1872-Feb. 26, 1885. 10 vols. 2 ft. 337
These letters continue in part the series described in entry 335. Arranged chronologically. Volumes 9-11 are indexed alphabetically by name of person, vessel, or subject. For registers, see entry 351.

LETTERS RECEIVED FROM THE COMMANDANT OF THE MARE ISLAND NAVY YARD. Apr. 24, 1872-Feb. 18, 1885. 8 vols. 2 ft. 338
These letters continue in part the series described in entry 335. Arranged chronologically. Volumes 6 and 7 are indexed alphabetically by name of person, vessel, or subject. For registers, see entry 351.

LETTERS RECEIVED FROM THE COMMANDANT OF THE NAVAL STATION AT MOUND CITY, ILL. Aug. 8, 1872-July 12, 1873. 1 vol. 3 in. 339
These letters continue in part the series described in entry 335. Arranged chronologically. For registers, see entry 351.

LETTERS RECEIVED FROM THE COMMANDANT OF THE NAVAL STATION AT NEW LONDON, CONN. Aug. 31, 1872-Dec. 20, 1883. 1 vol. 2 in. 340
These letters continue in part the series described in entry 335. Arranged chronologically. For registers, see entry 351.

LETTERS RECEIVED FROM THE COMMANDANT OF THE NEW YORK NAVY YARD. Apr. 30, 1872-Feb. 12, 1885. 9 vols. 2 ft. 341
These letters continue in part the series described in entry 335. Arranged chronologically. Volumes 7 and 8 are indexed alphabetically by name of person, vessel, or subject. For registers, see entry 351.

LETTERS RECEIVED FROM THE COMMANDANT OF THE NORFOLK NAVY YARD. Apr. 29, 1872-Feb. 26, 1885. 6 vols. 1 ft. 342
These letters continue in part the series described in entry 335. Arranged chronologically. Volume 5 is indexed alphabetically by name of person, vessel, or subject. For appropriate registers, see entry 351.

LETTERS RECEIVED FROM THE COMMANDANT OF THE PENSACOLA NAVY YARD.
May 2, 1872-Feb. 13, 1885. 3 vols. 6 in. 343
These letters continue in part the series described in entry 335.
Arranged chronologically. For registers, see entry 351.

LETTERS RECEIVED FROM THE COMMANDANT OF THE PHILADELPHIA NAVY YARD.
May 1, 1872-Nov. 24, 1875. 3 vols. 8 in. 344
These letters continue in part the series described in entry 335.
Arranged chronologically. For registers, see entry 351.

LETTERS RECEIVED FROM THE COMMANDANT OF THE NAVY YARD AT PORTSMOUTH,
N. H. Apr. 30, 1872-Feb. 25, 1885. 6 vols. 1 ft. 345
These letters continue in part the series described in entry 335.
Arranged chronologically. Volume 5 is indexed alphabetically by name of
person, vessel, or subject. For registers, see entry 351.

LETTERS RECEIVED FROM THE COMMANDANT OF THE NAVY YARD AT WASHINGTON,
D. C. May 1, 1872-Feb. 25, 1885. 16 vols. 4 ft. 346
These letters continue in part the series described in entry 335.
Arranged chronologically. Volumes 13-15 are indexed alphabetically by
name of person, vessel, or subject. For registers, see entry 351.

LETTERS RECEIVED FROM THE COMMANDING OFFICER OF THE TRAINING SQUADRONS
AND THE TRAINING STATION AT NEWPORT, R. I. May 24, 1881-Feb. 26,
1885. 3 vols. 8 in. 347
Letters and telegrams received that concern such matters as the recruiting, training, assignment, transfer, and allowance of apprentices
and other trainees; and housekeeping activities and routine reporting.
Arranged chronologically. Volume 1 is indexed alphabetically by name
of man, apprentice, vessel, or subject. For copies of letters sent to
the squadron for the same period, see entry 329. For registers, see
entry 351.

LETTERS RECEIVED FROM NAVY AGENTS AND PAY OFFICERS ("PAYMASTERS").
Nov. 4, 1862-Dec. 26, 1884. 11 vols. 3 ft. 348
Mainly letters and regular returns, accounts, statements, and reports
made by Navy pay agents and pay officers, including bills, vouchers,
exhibits, requisitions, contracts, certificates of deposit, monthly returns, and schedules of bids. A few telegrams are included. Arranged
chronologically. For registers, see entry 351. Copies of letters sent
to Navy agents and pay officers are described in entry 324.

LETTERS RECEIVED BY THE COMMANDING OFFICER OF THE NAVAL RENDEZVOUS AT
NEW YORK. Aug. 18, 1863-Apr. 20, 1865. 1 vol. 3 in. 349
Letters received, including some fair copies and copies of printed
orders. Most of the letters are from the Chief of the Bureau of Equipment and Recruiting, and from the Commandant of the New York Navy Yard.
Letters from the Bureau relate mainly to such enlistment matters as re-

ports and lists of men, correction of names in shipping articles, and improper enlistments; those from the Commandant of the New York Navy Yard are mainly in the form of orders. Arranged chronologically.

MISCELLANEOUS LETTERS RECEIVED. Oct. 6, 1862-Feb. 7, 1885; Oct. 19, 1889-Jan. 29, 1892. 298 vols. 56 ft. <u>350</u>

Some of the letters are in stub binders and some in permanently bound volumes, numbered, but with two volumes for each of the following: 270, 283, 284, 286, and 290. The series includes letters from other Government agencies and the public that are not readily assignable to other series. Arranged chronologically. A few volumes are indexed alphabetically by name of person and firm. Registers for the 1862-85 period are described in entry 351; for the 1885-90 period, in entry 353.

Indexes and Registers, 1862-90

REGISTERS OF LETTERS RECEIVED AND SENT. Sept. 1862-Dec. 1885. 27 vols. 7 ft. <u>351</u>

In these volumes the record of letters received is entered on the left-hand page and the record of letters sent, on the right-hand page. Opposite entries are not usually related. In early volumes only the dates and briefs of letters are given; in later volumes letter numbers are given, thus enabling the register to serve for series of letters received and both fair and press copies of letters sent by the Bureau. References to specific series and to volumes and page numbers are omitted. The volumes are divided into tabbed sections with such headings as follows: Secretary; Commandants (followed by tabbed section for each yard or station); Beaufort; Training Squadron; Public Printer; 4th Auditor; Commissioner of Pensions; Squadrons; Paymasters; Coast Survey; Stationery; C. G. & P. Ware (China, Glass and Plated Ware); Publishers; Officers; Miscellaneous; and Appendix. Arranged by year or group of years, thereunder by subject, and thereunder chronologically. References to these registers have been made in the descriptions of individual series of letters received and copies of letters sent. For registers and indexes to later correspondence received, see entries 353 and 354; for an index to letters sent, 1885-90, see entry 352.

INDEX TO LETTERS SENT. 1885-90. 6 vols. 2 ft. <u>352</u>

This is an index by name of correspondent or ship or by subject, arranged alphabetically by the first two letters, as "Ba" and "Be." Opposite each name is a brief of the letter, together with a number and letter, as "233C," designating page 233 of volume C of the correspondence described in entry 279. Letters for the year 1890 are indexed, although the letters themselves are missing. Registers that serve as an index to letters sent, 1862-85, are described in entry 351.

RECORD OF LETTERS RECEIVED. Jan. 1885-Oct. 1890. 11 vols. 3 ft. <u>353</u>

These volumes continue, in part, those described in entry 351. The same general arrangement is maintained in that information on letters received is given on the left-hand page and information on letters sent and action taken, on the right-hand page. The entries are arranged chronologically in these volumes and each letter received has a number. The numbering was begun again each year so that the entries are arranged both chronologically and numerically. An alphabetical index supplementing this series is described in entry 354.

INDEX TO LETTERS RECEIVED. 1885-90. 6 vols. 2 ft.   354
In these volumes, one to a year, letters are entered alphabetically by the initial two letters of name of person, firm, vessel, or subject. Each entry consists of the name or subject, followed by a letter number and a brief of the contents. Since page and series references are not given, letters must be located with the help of the letter number. More complete information on the letters received and action taken thereon may be had by referring to the numerically arranged series described in entry 353. For an index to letters sent by this Bureau for the same period, see entry 352.

REGISTER TO LETTERS RECEIVED AND SENT RELATING TO EQUIPMENT AND COMPLEMENTS OF VESSELS. Jan. 1884-Mar. 1885. 1 vol. 3 in.   355
In this volume the entries for letters received are on the left-hand pages and for letters sent, on the right-hand pages. The letter numbers, dates, and subjects are shown. Opposite entries appear to be unrelated. Arranged alphabetically by name of ship and thereunder chronologically.

INDEX TO CORRESPONDENCE CONCERNING ENLISTED MEN AND APPRENTICES. 1887-89. 1 vol. 3 in.   356
This volume contains two sections; the first section is arranged alphabetically by subject, and the second, alphabetically by name of enlisted man or apprentice. The entries contain references to numbers of the letters sent that are described in entry 279 and to numbers of the letters received that have not been identified.

Reports of Conduct and Shipping Articles, 1857-1910

QUARTERLY REPORTS OF CONDUCT OF ENLISTED MEN AND BOYS ("CONDUCT BOOK," "PROGRESS OF BOYS"). Apr. 1875-June 1889. 82 vols. 11 ft.   357
These volumes contain the following types of conduct reports: (1) "Conduct Report of the Crew of the U.S.S. _____, for the Quarter ending ____ day of ____, 18__," which shows the man's name, rating, age, occupation, usual place of residence, previous naval service, scores for professional qualifications, conduct, leaves of absence, liberty, and punishments; and (2) "Report of Progress, Aptitude, Conduct, &c., of Apprentices on Board the U.S.S. _____ for the Quarter Ending _____, 18__," which shows the apprentice's name, rating, date and place of enlistment, date of expiration of enlistment, date he was received on board, class, scores made in apprentice subjects, number of times he was reported for misconduct, punishments inflicted, and remarks. Arranged alphabeti-

cally by name of ship, thereunder chronologically, and thereunder in general alphabetically by name of man or boy. For another series of conduct reports combined with duplicate shipping articles, see entry 358.

REPORTS OF CONDUCT OF ENLISTED MEN AND DUPLICATES OF COMPOSITE SHIPPING ARTICLES ("CONDUCT BOOK," "CONDUCT BOOK AND DUPLICATE SHIPPING ARTICLES"). 1867-1910. 989 vols. 83 ft. 358

The conduct reports and the duplicate shipping articles, which begin about August 1896, are bound together to form one series. There are two types of conduct records: (1) conduct records of individuals, and (2) summary conduct records. Conduct records of individuals are on printed forms, submitted quarterly, each showing the man's name and rating, date and place of enlistment, term of enlistment, previous naval service, certificates of honorable discharge and continuous service, good conduct badges, marital status, personal description, place or vessel from which received, and date received. Summary conduct records, which were also submitted quarterly, show name of man, professional qualifications (proficiency, seamanship, gunnery), conduct (industry, obedience, cleanliness), average standing calculated on an 0-5 numerical scale, state of health, offenses, punishments, state of accounts, and other data. The composite shipping articles are printed forms and constitute a contract between the commanding officer of the ship and the men enlisted. They contain enlistment, vital, medical, and other information described in greater detail in entries 359 and 360. Arranged alphabetically by name of ship and thereunder chronologically. Conduct records are indexed alphabetically by name of ship and thereunder chronologically; shipping articles are not indexed. For another series of conduct reports, 1875-89, see entry 357.

COMPOSITE SHIPPING ARTICLES OF ENLISTED MEN ON NAVAL VESSELS. Jan. 1857-Dec. 1884. 71 vols. 6 ft. 359

Printed forms, each of which constitutes a contract between the commanding officer of the ship and the men listed on the form. On the form are shown the name of the commanding officer, name and rate of ship, term of man's enlistment, date of enlistment, recruit's signature or "mark," name as written in by an officer, rating, wages per month, amount of wages advanced, bounty paid, signatures of sureties for wages advanced and bounty paid, and signature of witness to recruit's signature. Arranged by ship and thereunder chronologically. For a separate index, see entry 361. For other shipping articles, see entries 358 and 360.

COMPOSITE SHIPPING ARTICLES OF APPRENTICES ON NAVAL VESSELS. 1864-84. 8 vols. 3 ft. 360

Agreements between naval officers and boys for the latter to serve until they reach the age of 21. The agreement shows for each apprentice the date of enlistment, name, rating, wages per month, term of service, signature, signatures of parents or guardians, and signature of witness.

Arranged by name of ship or recruiting place and thereunder chronologically. For a separate index, see entry 361.

INDEX TO COMPOSITE SHIPPING ARTICLES. 1861-84. 1 vol. 1 in. 361

Shows the dates for which shipping articles were submitted for each vessel. Arranged alphabetically by initial letter of name of vessel or recruiting place and thereunder by date of shipping article. This volume indexes in part the shipping articles described in entries 359 and 360.

Records Concerning Discharges and Desertions, 1856-89

QUARTERLY RETURNS OF DESERTERS FROM NAVAL VESSELS ("REPORT OF DESERTERS"). July 28, 1863-Dec. 31, 1885. 47 vols. 7 ft. 362

These volumes contain letters and enclosed lists (later printed forms) signed by commanding officers of ships. They show the deserter's name, rating, date and place of enlistment, place of birth, age, description, date of desertion, reward offered for apprehension, statement of account (balance due the deserter or amount overpaid), and remarks. In volumes 1-12 the reports are numbered, but no key or index is available. In volumes 13-47 the reports are arranged alphabetically by name of vessel, and thereunder chronologically, if there is more than one report per vessel in the same volume. Volumes 43-47 are indexed alphabetically by name of vessel.

RECORD OF DESERTERS. Jan. 1, 1867-Mar. 26, 1889. 4 vols. 7 in. 363

These volumes give the deserter's name, rating, date of desertion, ship or station deserted from, amount of pay due or overpaid, reward offered, and remarks. Arranged alphabetically by initial letter of deserter's name and thereunder chronologically.

COPIES OF HONORABLE DISCHARGES AND RELATED RECORDS ("HONORABLE DISCHARGES"). Jan. 1, 1864-Aug. 29, 1878. 35 vols. 6 ft. 364

In addition to copies of honorable discharges, these "stub binders" contain discharge certificates, descriptive lists of men, and correspondence relating to men eligible for discharge. Arranged chronologically. About a third of the volumes are indexed by initial letter of name of man and vessel. For separate indexes to volumes 1-31, see entry 365.

INDEX TO HONORABLE DISCHARGES. ca. 1856-Jan. 1875. 3 vols. 10 in.
365

These volumes list the man's name, rating, and vessel, with a reference to the volume and page number of the series of honorable discharges described in entry 364 (vols. 1-31 only). They also serve as an index to discharge papers for the period 1856-64 that are missing. Entries are arranged by initial two or three letters of name of man discharged.

PRESS COPIES OF CERTIFICATES OF HONORABLE DISCHARGE. June 2, 1865-
Jan. 12, 1871. 1 vol. 2 in. 366
These are copies of the filled-in portions of honorable discharge
certificates issued by the Bureau. This series is duplicated in part
by the copies described in entry 364. Arranged chronologically. The
volume is indexed by initial letter of name of man discharged.

FAIR COPIES OF CERTIFICATES OF HONORABLE DISCHARGE. June 2, 1865-
Feb. 3, 1870. 1 vol. 2 in. 367
These copies of completed certificates duplicate those described in
entry 366, except for the difference in terminal date, and are similarly
arranged and indexed.

PRESS COPIES OF DISCHARGE ORDERS ISSUED TO COMMANDING OFFICERS ASHORE
AND AFLOAT ("DISCHARGES"). Feb. 4, 1864-Feb. 28, 1885. 22 vols.
3 ft. 368
Orders to commanding officers of squadrons, vessels, yards, and stations to discharge men from naval service. Arranged chronologically.
Most of the volumes are indexed alphabetically by initial letter of
name of person to be discharged. The fair copies described in entry
369 duplicate part of these orders.

FAIR COPIES OF DISCHARGE ORDERS ISSUED TO COMMANDING OFFICERS ASHORE
AND AFLOAT ("DISCHARGES"). Feb. 4, 1864-July 29, 1874; Jan. 4, 1882-
Dec. 31, 1883. 3 vols. 8 in. 369
These copies duplicate in part those described in entry 368 and are
similarly arranged and indexed.

Continuous-Service Certificates and Records Relating to Merit Awards, 1863-1928

CORRESPONDENCE AND REPORTS RELATING TO CONTINUOUS-SERVICE CERTIFICATES.
Aug. 1867-Aug. 1880. 17 vols. 3 ft. 370
These stub binders contain lists of men either holding or recommended
for continuous-service certificates and descriptive, biographical, and
service information concerning them; letters of transmittal; and, occasionally, certificates of honorable discharge. Numbered serially
1-3917. Arranged in general chronologically. For a series of continuous-
service certificates, 1865-99, see entry 223. Some continuous-service
certificates of enlisted men are described in entry 232.

RECORD OF AWARD OF GOOD CONDUCT BADGES. June 1870-Dec. 1874. 6 vols.
8 in. 371
Contain name of recipient, vessel served on, and a name and date that
are probably the name of the officer recommending the award and the date
on which he made the recommendation. Arranged alphabetically by initial
two letters of name of man receiving the badge. For Bureau of Navigation
correspondence relating to such badges, see entry 69.

RECORD OF CERTIFICATES OF COMMENDATION. 1879-85. 1 vol. 1 in.   372
Contains certificate number, name of recipient, date of enlistment, rate, continuous-service certificate number, and, under remarks, a surname and date that are probably the name of the recommending officer and the date on which recommendation of the award was made. Arranged alphabetically by initial letter of recipient's name.

RECORD OF MEDAL OF HONOR AWARDS. 1863-1928. 1 vol. 2 in.   372-A
Contains names of individuals awarded the Medal of Honor during the period 1863-1928. (Dates on the binding of the volume are erroneously printed as 1861-1924.) Included are citations as well as notations regarding delivery of the medals, their acceptance, and the like. A number of extracts from statutes authorizing the awards are at the front of the volume. Arranged chronologically. The volume is indexed alphabetically by name of recipient.

Records Relating to Naval Apprentices, 1880-86

These records are series that were begun by the Bureau of Equipment and Recruiting but were not continued by the Bureau of Navigation when supervision of the apprentice-training system was returned to it in 1889. The history of the training system and most of the records relating to apprentices are described on pages 71-75.

REGISTER OF QUARTERLY EXAMINATION OF BOYS ON BOARD THE U.S.S. SHENANDOAH. Nov. 6, 1883-Oct. 23, 1886. 1 vol. 1/2 in.   373
Shows grades received in seamanship, signaling, gunnery, academic subjects, and conduct as well as other information concerning special aptitudes and abilities of the apprentices. Arranged alphabetically by name of apprentice; all grades given each boy are listed chronologically thereunder. The volume is indexed alphabetically by initial letter of name.

RECORDS RELATING TO THE ESTABLISHMENT OF A HEADQUARTERS FOR TRAINING NAVAL APPRENTICES. Nov. 27, 1880-Apr. 2, 1883. 1 vol. 1/2 in.
   374
Copies of correspondence concerning proposed sites for a headquarters, including reports and legal documents relating to the acquisition of Coasters Harbor Island by the State of Rhode Island from the city of Newport, with a view to its transfer to the U. S. Government for use as a naval training school for apprentices. Unarranged.

Other Records, 1906

LISTS OF RECORDS OF THE BUREAU OF EQUIPMENT AND RECRUITING THAT WERE TURNED OVER TO THE BUREAU OF NAVIGATION BY THE BUREAU OF EQUIPMENT. ca. 1906. 1/2 in.   375
This series consists of two lists, one showing the series of letters transferred (sent and received, ca. 1862-85) and one, titled "Keys,"

showing the location by locker number of various types of records (ca. 1885-1903). The first list is arranged by letters received and sent, thereunder by source of records or by series; the second list is arranged by type of record, thereunder by locker number, room, and case number.

RECORD OF COMPLEMENTS OF VESSELS. n.d. 1 vol. 2 in. 376
Relates to the armament and complement of officers and men on naval vessels. Arranged in general alphabetically by name of vessel and thereunder by rank. The volume is indexed alphabetically by name of vessel.

RECORDS OF DIVISIONS OF THE BUREAU OF NAVIGATION, 1804-1946

Records of the Chaplains Division, 1804-1946

Since the date of its establishment in 1798, the Navy Department has made provision for chaplains to conduct divine services. The number of chaplains, however, remained small until the United States entered World War I. In 1842 the limit was placed at 24 and this number was not increased until 1914. In 1917 there was 59 chaplains and at the close of the war, 199. During 1917, when the Chaplain Corps was undergoing a rapid expansion, the need for central administration was met by assigning a chaplain of many years' experience, Capt. John Brown Frazier, as the first Chief of the Chaplains Division in the Bureau of Navigation. He supervised the Chaplain Corps and had charge of the selection of candidates proposed by the Federal Council of the Churches of Christ in America, representing the Protestant denominations, and the Military Ordinariate of the Roman Catholic Church. More than half of the chaplains resigned immediately after the war ended, leaving an insufficient number to serve the Navy. In 1934 the Navy Department Board on Reorganization recommended a strength of 76 chaplains for the corps. Most of the records of the World War II period have been retained by the Bureau of Naval Personnel; those described below represent in only a limited way the greatly expanded activities of chaplains in that period. The story of the Chaplain Corps is told by Clifford M. Drury in The History of the Chaplain Corps (Bureau of Naval Personnel, 1949. 2 vols.).

GENERAL CORRESPONDENCE. 1916-40. 8 ft. 377
Mainly correspondence of the Division, but including some routine reports, blank forms, sermons, processed questionnaires, and filled-in forms (some as late as 1944). Among the subjects covered are bible societies, casualties, Catholic Church, chapels, Chaplain's Association, discipline, Episcopal Church, examining boards, flags, Fleet Service, funerals, grievances, life insurance, Methodist Episcopal Church, policy, procurement, selections, training, war plans, welfare, and YMCA. Arranged alphabetically by subject and thereunder chronologically; a small quantity of miscellaneous processed and printed material is unarranged.

RECORDS CONTAINING BIOGRAPHICAL, SERVICE-RECORD, AND OTHER DATA ABOUT
 CHAPLAINS. 1804-1923. 7 ft. <u>378</u>
 This series includes the following subseries: (1) jackets containing
correspondence with or about chaplains; (2) biographical and service-
record information concerning chaplains; and (3) copies of replies to
inquiries concerning chaplains. Most of the subseries are arranged
alphabetically by name of chaplain; the remaining material is unarranged.

MISCELLANEOUS RECORDS RELATING TO CHAPLAINS. 1898-1946. 9 ft. <u>379</u>
 This series includes unit histories of ships and stations in both
narrative and photographic form, some of which are published; smooth
logs of the Chaplains School at Williamsburg, Va.; cruise records; news
releases and other publicity materials; form letters concerning certificates of appreciation awarded to churches whose ministers had entered
the Chaplain Corps; and miscellaneous printed and processed matter.
Records in this series document an important phase of the history of
chaplains in the Navy--their struggle to obtain proper recognition,
rights, and understanding from the public. Arranged in part alphabetically within subseries.

PICTORIAL RECORDS RELATING TO CHAPLAINS. 1917-45. 9 ft. <u>380</u>
 Consist of 11 oil portraits of prominent chaplains who served during
the period 1811-43; 36 panel frames (each containing 10 photographs of
chaplains); 1 group photograph; 11 framed items, including mottoes,
photographs, and posters; 2 memorial plaques to noted chaplains, apparently intended to be affixed to the Chidwick and Royce Memorial
Chapels; and miscellaneous photographs relating to chaplains' activities.
These records are part of a collection of historical material relating
to chaplains, which was assembled by William Wilcox Edel, USN (Ret.).
Unarranged.

"THE PEACEMAKERS." May 30, 1945. 1 16-in. sound recording. <u>381</u>
 This is a sound recording of a Navy Department program, recorded by
the National Broadcasting Co. for release on Memorial Day, 1945, in
commemoration of the war dead of the Navy, Coast Guard, and Marine Corps.

<u>Records of the Division of Naval Militia Affairs, 1891-1918</u>

Until December 1, 1909, administrative matters relating to Naval
Militia of the various States were handled by the Assistant Secretary
of the Navy, but on that date they were transferred to the Personnel
Division of the Office of the Secretary. As early as March 1891 Congress
appropriated $25,000 for arms and equipment for the State Naval Militia,
and in August 1894 it authorized the loan of old naval vessels to them
for training purposes. During the Spanish-American War 4,316 men of the
Naval Militia served with the regular Navy, the Auxiliary Naval Force,
and the Coast Signal Service. In 1911 the Office of Naval Militia was
established in the Personnel Division of the Office of the Secretary of
the Navy.

In 1912 functions relating to Naval Militia affairs were placed under the Bureau of Navigation. The Naval Militia Act of February 16, 1914 (38 Stat. 283), defined the increased powers and responsibilities of the Navy Department in relation to the Naval Militia of the States, Territories, and the District of Columbia. On April 12 of that year the Division of Naval Militia Affairs was established in the Bureau by Navy Department General Order No. 93. The Naval Reserve Force was authorized by an act of Congress of August 29, 1916, which also provided for the enrollment of the Naval Militia in time of war into a force to be known as the National Naval Volunteers. At the outbreak of war with Germany nearly all the militia volunteered for enrollment in the latter organization, so that the Federal Government found itself with two organizations--the Naval Reserve Force, recruited mainly from ex-service men and the merchant marine, and the National Naval Volunteers, composed of the former State Naval Militias--maintained for the purpose of reinforcing the Navy in time of war. On July 1, 1918, all laws relating to the Naval Militia and the National Naval Volunteers were repealed and the President was authorized to transfer the personnel of the latter to the Naval Reserve Force. The Division of Naval Militia Affairs was then discontinued.

GENERAL RECORDS. 1891-1918. 56 ft.   382

These records are almost completely disarranged, but the following types of records are identifiable: (1) correspondence with Navy bureaus, local and State Naval Militia, and vessels, relating to summer cruises, the Naval Reserve, and housekeeping matters; (2) routine reports, such as Naval Militia Survey and Appraisals of Title "B" Equipage; (3) affidavits for lost property, made by officers and men of the Naval Militia and sent to the Division; (4) circulars; (5) copies of rules and regulations governing local militia organizations in the States; (6) record cards for Naval Militia officers; and (7) six small volumes containing messages sent between vessels. The correspondence is arranged according to one or more numerical systems; part of the other records are arranged alphabetically by name of vessel, person, or subject.

CARD INDEX TO CORRESPONDENCE. 1903-10. 2 ft.   383

These cards are evidently an index to part of the correspondence described in entry 382. The disarrangement of most of such correspondence, however, makes it impossible to state with any certainty to what part this index applies. The cards contain numeric-subject symbols but the corresponding subjects are in most instances not given. Cards for the year 1906 are an exception, and illustrations of the symbols used and the corresponding subjects are as follows: 1-P, Returns of Strength; 19-P, Returns Stores; 41-P, Orders, R. I.; 110-P, Allotment Made; 141-P, All Surveys; and 168-P, Annual Returns. Many of the classification symbols stand for vessels, as "51-P--Parts for Oriole's launch." Dates and briefs of letters appear on these cards in chronological order. The cards are arranged by year, thereunder by symbol, and thereunder by number.

LETTERS SENT. Oct. 5, 1911. 53 vols. 5 ft.   384

Press copies of letters, telegrams, and endorsements sent during the period when the administration of Naval Militia affairs was successively in the office of the Assistant Secretary and in the Personnel Division of the Secretary's Office. The first 8 volumes are almost illegible; 14 others are labeled "N. M." and "Department"; and most of the others contain copies of letters sent to States having Naval Militia. All except the last group of letters are arranged chronologically; letters to States are arranged by State and thereunder chronologically. The volumes are indexed alphabetically by subject, name, or State.

REPORTS OF STATE NAVAL MILITIA ORGANIZATIONS. 1913-15. 4 in.   385

Annual reports for the fiscal years 1914 and 1915, on Form N. N. M. 18, showing instruction given during the year to the Naval Militia organization in each State, excepting summer exercises on Navy vessels and target practice. There are separate reports for each battalion, division, or other unit on such matters as drilling and summer cruises. Arranged by State and thereunder by type of report. There is a small quantity of unarranged material.

SUMMARIES OF THE ENROLLED FORCE OF NAVAL MILITIA UNITS. 1915-16. 2 in.
   386

These summaries, on Form N. Nav. 109-D, contain muster-roll information from vessels used by the Naval Militia during fiscal year 1916. Some of the forms contain information from such shore units as the Naval Hospital at New York and the Navy Receiving Station at Richmond. The series also includes two muster rolls on regular muster-roll forms for the Wasp and a few miscellaneous lists and transmittal letters. The records are arranged alphabetically by name of vessel or shore unit.

PAYROLL OF THE THIRD BATTALION, NEW YORK NAVAL MILITIA. Aug. 13-26,
   1915. 1 vol. 1/2 in.   387

This paperbacked volume contains S. and A. Form 1, "Pay Roll of the United States _____ Pay _____, U. S. Navy. From _____, 191_, to _____, 191_." During this pay period the Third Battalion was assigned to the Kearsarge. The date stamp on the back of the volume contains the words "Naval Militia . . . Navy Department." Names are entered by rank and thereunder by pay number.

CERTIFICATES OF QUALIFICATION FOR NAVAL MILITIA RATINGS. July 6-Dec. 9,
   1916. 1 vol. 2 in.   388

These are printed copies of certificates of qualification, the originals of which were signed by the Chief of the Division of Naval Militia Affairs and by the Secretary of the Navy. These certificates were applicable only to ratings in the Naval Militia. Arranged and indexed alphabetically by name of person.

ALLOWANCE BOOKS FOR VESSELS USED BY THE NAVAL MILITIA. 1912-17.
26 vols. 2 ft. <u>389</u>

Contain blueprint copies of allowances for vessels used by the Naval Militia, with one volume for each vessel. There are sections showing the allowance to each bureau under various appropriations, chiefly "Equipment of Vessels." The volumes are unarranged, but within each volume the copies of allowances are arranged by appropriation and thereunder by bureau.

ORDNANCE ALLOWANCE BOOKS. 1915-16. 20 vols. 2 ft. <u>390</u>

Show ordnance allowances to units of the Naval Militia. The series also includes three volumes of miscellaneous material such as bulletins, mailing lists, and stencil forms. Arranged by State and thereunder by town where the Naval Militia unit was located.

REPORT OF ANNUAL CONVENTION OF THE NATIONAL NAVAL MILITIA ASSOCIATION.
Jan. 28 and 29, 1916. 1 vol. 1/2 in. <u>391</u>

This bound volume contains what is apparently a verbatim transcript (typed) of notes taken during the convention and a list of State representatives. Arranged by session.

Records of the Division of Officers and Fleet, 1887-98

In March 1861 an Office of Detail was established in the Secretary's Office to handle matters relating to the appointment and detailing of officers, and in 1865 it was placed under the supervision of the Chief of the Bureau of Navigation. In 1889 it was formally transferred to the Bureau and was renamed the Division of Officers and Fleet.

Records of the Office of Detail were maintained separately and are described on pages 79-83 of this inventory. There is, however, some overlapping of dates in records attributed to the two units, since some series that were begun by the Office but that were discontinued soon after the Division was established are described with records of the Office. Other records, particularly those series of correspondence begun in January 1887 when the system of folding correspondence and filing it in document containers was inaugurated, are described below. For the period 1890-95 copies of letters sent by the Division are a part of the general correspondence of the Bureau, chief among which are orders sent to officers, 1890-96 (entry 48) and letters sent to officers, 1890-96 (entry 46). After July 1895 they were, for the most part, filed with the related letters received.

Certain operational files have been removed from the correspondence of the Division for inclusion in the Naval Records Collection of the Office of Naval Records and Library, Record Group 45.

LETTERS RECEIVED. 1887-95. 191 ft. <u>392</u>

Letters received by the "Detail Division" in the Secretary's Office from January 1887 to July 1889, and after that by the Division of Officers and Fleet. They are numbered serially, with a new series of numbers for each year through 1890 and one continuous series for the period 1891-95. The letters include requests for and acknowledgments of orders; requests for delays in reporting and for change of detail; reports concerning health, discharges from hospitals, and duty assignments; and lists of officers. Arranged chronologically and thereunder by serial number. For registers, see entries 277 and 394.

GENERAL CORRESPONDENCE. 1895-97. 30 ft. 393
This correspondence is similar to that described in entry 392 except that it contains copies of letters sent. Miscellaneous reports on tactics and movements of vessels, received from the U. S. Naval Force, North Atlantic Station, are at the end of the series. Arranged chronologically and thereunder by number. For registers, see entry 394.

REGISTERS OF CORRESPONDENCE ("ABSTRACT OF CORRESPONDENCE"). Jan. 1891-Feb. 1896. 14 vols. 3 ft. 394
For letters received the following information is recorded: number of letter, date written and date received, writer's name, and a brief of the contents. Under "Action and Letters Sent" are the date of reply, name of addressee, a brief of the letter's contents, and a reference to the series, volume, and page number of the volume containing a press copy of the letter. Entries are for the most part chronological under the name of the administrative unit (vessel, yard, station, or bureau) of the Navy Department or of the other Government agency with which correspondence was exchanged. The volumes are arranged by alphabetical designation. For earlier registers, see entry 277.

APPOINTMENTS OF PAYMASTERS' CLERKS. 1889-91. 1 ft. 395
This series consists mainly of copies of a folded form containing the notice of appointment, agreement to abide by authority of the Navy Department, and oath. Many of the appointments are stamped "Division of Officers and Fleet." They are numbered and arranged in accordance with such numbers. In addition, they are numbered as part of the series of letters received (see entry 392). For a register covering the 1889-90 period, see entry 277.

ACCEPTANCES OF APPOINTMENTS AS PAYMASTERS' CLERKS. 1891-98. 11 in. 396
This series consists mainly of jackets containing such material as acceptance forms, oaths, letters of recommendation, and notices to appear before a Naval Examining Board. Numbered as a part of the correspondence of the Division and arranged in accordance with such numbers. For registers, see entry 394.

LISTS OF NAVAL, MARINE, AND CIVIL OFFICERS AND ATTACHÉS OF YARDS AND STATIONS. Jan. 1890-Dec. 1894. 5 vols. 1 ft. 397
These are monthly lists of officers at naval yards and stations, in-

cluding receiving ships. They are listed under such headings as Commandant's Office, Bureau of Yards and Docks, other bureaus of the Navy Department, Marine barracks, receiving ship, and Office of Purchasing and Disbursing Paymaster. Arranged by year, thereunder alphabetically by name of yard or station, and thereunder chronologically. For other lists of officers, see entries 180-188.

Records of the Naval Academy Division, 1851-1940

The Bureau of Ordnance and Hydrography was the first Navy bureau vested with responsibility for administration of the Naval Academy. In 1862 the Academy was placed under the newly created Bureau of Navigation. Exactly when the Naval Academy Division was created has not been ascertained. Except for the correspondence of the Superintendent of the Academy while it was under the Bureau of Ordnance and Hydrography (entry 398), the following records are those of what is sometimes described as the "Naval Academy Section," sometimes as the "Naval Academy Division" of the Bureau of Navigation. From 1869 to 1889 this Bureau had no connection with the affairs of the Academy but such records as fall within those years may, like those of the Bureau of Ordnance and Hydrography, be considered Bureau of Navigation records through inheritance.

GENERAL CORRESPONDENCE OF THE SUPERINTENDENT OF THE NAVAL ACADEMY.
   July 1, 1851-Oct. 28, 1853; Apr. 17, 1855-Oct. 20, 1858. 4 vols.
   6 in.   398
   Relates to the general administration of the Academy and consists of letters received by and copies of letters sent to the Chief of the Bureau of Ordnance and Hydrography. Volumes 1 and 5 are missing. Arranged chronologically. The index in each volume gives the date and a brief of each letter.

CORRESPONDENCE RELATING TO APPLICANTS FOR APPOINTMENT AS NAVAL CADETS
   AT LARGE ("REGISTERS"). June 1863-May 1892. 8 ft.   399
   These applicants were not admitted to the Naval Academy. Appointments "at large" could be made by the Secretary of the Navy for congressional districts whose Congressmen did not submit nominations for naval cadets. The correspondence is numbered serially, 501-3494. Arranged chronologically.

CORRESPONDENCE RELATING TO APPLICANTS FOR ADMISSION TO THE NAVAL ACADEMY. 1862-78; Aug. 1891-Jan. 1896. 8 ft.   400
   A part of the correspondence, including some miscellaneous material, is for the earlier period, 1862-78, and bears no serial numbers. Most of the correspondence is for the later period, 1891-96, and bears the serial numbers 840-5900. The earlier records are unarranged; the later ones are arranged chronologically. The registers described in entry 401 may be useful as a guide to the later records.

REGISTERS OF CORRESPONDENCE ("ABSTRACT OF CORRESPONDENCE"). Jan. 1, 1891-Dec. 31, 1895. 2 vols. 5 in. 401

Contain the following information: (1) for letters received, name of writer, place from which letter was sent, date of letter, date of its receipt, number assigned to letter, and a brief of its contents; and (2) for letters sent, date of letter, a brief of its contents or a notation of action taken, and a reference to the volume and page number of the series of press copies containing a copy of the letters. A separate section of the registers contains correspondence of the Superintendent of the Academy. Each volume is indexed alphabetically by name of correspondent or subject. The series of press copies referred to are among those described in entries 1-71.

LETTERS OF APPOINTMENT ISSUED TO NAVAL CADETS AND MIDSHIPMEN ("APPOINTMENTS, NAVAL CADETS"). May 1894-Nov. 1940. 12 vols. 3 ft. 402

These are copies of formal appointment letters from the Secretary of the Navy. Each letter shows date of issuance and effective date of appointment, name of appointee, and congressional district from which appointed. The first appointments were made on May 27, 1894, the latest on November 4, 1940. Arranged chronologically by dates the Secretary signed the appointments. The volumes contain alphabetical name indexes.

JACKETS OF NAVAL CADETS. Nov. 1862-July 1910. 164 ft. 403

These jackets contain a letter of nomination from a Congressman, the candidate's letter of acceptance, testimonial letters, reports of examining and medical boards, oaths, papers and reports relating to discipline, copies of orders and acknowledgments thereof, letters relating to the cadet's promotion to ensign, and other papers. Most of the candidates represented by these jackets failed in examinations, resigned, or were dismissed for disciplinary reasons. The jackets bear notations conveying a part of the information in the records enclosed and a number. Arranged and numbered (2-9132) in general chronologically by date of admission for examination.

REGISTER OF MIDSHIPMEN. 1869-76. 1 vol. 3 in. 404

Contains a list of midshipmen that shows, for each man, personal data, name of Congressman recommending him, dates "permitted" and appointed, and notations as to whether he was dropped, graduated, or the like. Arranged in general by serial or jacket number. The volume contains an alphabetical name index.

RECORDS OF GRADUATIONS AND RESIGNATIONS OF CADET MIDSHIPMEN. Mar. 1869-Sept. 1873. 1 vol. 1/2 in. 405

The volume contains copies of the form titled "Cadet Midshipmen," which gives the following information: manner of appointment, name of midshipman, his class, date of appointment, and remarks. In the front of the volume are listed the names of men appointed "At Large by the President"; the remainder of the volume is arranged alphabetically by name of State from which the man was appointed and thereunder by name of appointee.

MONTHLY REPORTS OF EXAMINATIONS AND STANDINGS AT THE NAVAL ACADEMY.
June 1870-Apr. 1888. 3 vols. 8 in. 406

These volumes contain copies of the forms titled "Report of Examination" and "Report of the Relative Standing of the members of the _____ class." The examination report was also used to indicate persons who failed or were to be replaced for other reasons. Arranged chronologically by month and thereunder by class.

REPORTS OF ANNUAL EXAMINATIONS, STANDINGS, AND MERIT ROLLS AT THE
NAVAL ACADEMY. 1879-81; 1884-88. 1 ft. 407

Consist of three types of reports: general merit rolls or merit rolls for a particular class; reports of relative standings of members of a class; and reports showing cadets found deficient and recommended for reexamination or dropping. Arranged by year, thereunder by class, and thereunder by type of examination (Cadet Engineer, Cadet Midshipman, and the like).

QUARTERLY FITNESS REPORTS OF MIDSHIPMEN. 1900-1910. 20 ft. 408

These are printed forms (N. Nav. G), folded in jackets, that were signed by the commanding officer. They contain the following information: name of midshipman; division; ship to which attached; nature of duties; ability; attention to duty; manner of performing duties; zeal, intelligence, and judgment in instructing, drilling, and handling enlisted men; general conduct and bearing; health; duties other than ordinary routine; use of liquor, if any; punishments; and remarks. Arranged alphabetically by name of midshipman.

RECORDS OF RESERVE OFFICERS' CLASSES AT THE NAVAL ACADEMY. 1917-19.
2 in. 409

This series consists of sheets that were apparently taken from a looseleaf binder. They contain lists of officers, minutes of council meetings, recommendations as to assignments, grades, instruction schedules, curricula, and related correspondence. Arranged by subject and preceded by an alphabetical index.

Records of the Morale Division, 1918-24

The Morale Division, called the Sixth Division until 1921, was an outgrowth of the work of the Navy Department Commission on Training Camp Activities, which was organized on July 26, 1917, to maintain morale, to supply recreation to men in training, and to handle problems of liquor and vice. The Commission's work covered three areas--law enforcement, inside camp activities and the Fleet, and outside or shore activities. It worked through existing law enforcement, social, recreational, and welfare organizations. At its meeting in January 1919 the Commission recommended to the Secretary of the Navy that its work be taken over by a division set up for that purpose in the Bureau of Navigation. As a result, the Sixth Division was set up by authority of Bureau of Navigation Circular Letter No. 33-19 of March 11, 1919, "to aid constituted authority to maintain a high morale." Its functions, according to the Secretary's report for 1919, were "to aid commanding officers in maintaining the morale of their commands; first, by ministering to the comfort, contentment, and recreation of the officers and men; second, by careful study of the great problems which affect the contentment of the Navy; third, by dealing with complaints of every nature from the service."

At first the work of the Division was carried on mainly by experienced civilian welfare specialists from such organizations as the American National Red Cross, the YMCA, and the YWCA, but gradually and systematically these specialists were replaced by enlisted and commissioned personnel of the Navy. Activities of the Division were at first confined mainly to shore stations but were soon expanded to vessels of the Fleet. Every vessel and shore station eventually had an officer especially detailed as an aide for morale. From 1920 on morale activities were decentralized more and more by distributing the bulk of the appropriation for "Recreation for Enlisted Men" in the form of allotments to ships and stations to be administered by their commanding officers. Naval hospitals were given a special allotment and, in addition, the Division maintained trained librarians at each of the larger hospitals. Occupational therapy became an important feature of this hospital work. Ships stores were also made available to the men and the profits realized from these sales were used to supplement the funds regularly allocated.

In 1923 the Morale Division was transferred to the Training Division and was reestablished as the Welfare and Recreation Section of that Division. Capt. C. R. Train, who had been head of the Morale Division, was made its chief. Records of the Training Division are described in entries 417-424.

GENERAL CORRESPONDENCE. 1918-20. 18 ft. 410
Pertains to such subjects as athletics, relations with bureaus of the Navy Department, chaplains, entertainment and recreation, the fleets, law enforcement, libraries, morale, recruiting, ships and stations, social hygiene, and welfare organizations. There is a small quantity of miscellaneous correspondence, some as early as 1906, together with circulars, pamphlets, reports, and other items. Arranged mainly by a numerical system the key to which is printed on each folder.

GENERAL CORRESPONDENCE OF THE MORALE AND RECREATION SECTION. 1920-24.
2 ft. 411
Mainly letters received, preceded by several folders of copies of letters sent, relating to typical morale matters under such headings as advertisements, clubs, instructions, memoranda and circular letters, motion pictures, recreation and athletics, recruiting, and service newspapers. Arranged alphabetically by subject or name and thereunder chronologically. There is some overlapping between this correspondence and that of the Welfare and Recreation Section of the Training Division, which is described in entry 422.

CORRESPONDENCE WITH FOREIGN STATIONS. 1920. 2 ft. 412
Relates to matters of morale at foreign stations, such as allotments, requests for recreational or club facilities, equipment, libraries, desertions, social hygiene, and other subjects having to do with the mental and physical well-being of Navy enlisted and officer personnel. Arranged alphabetically by station and thereunder alphabetically by subject.

CORRESPONDENCE RELATING TO PORTS. 1918-20. 10 in. 413
This correspondence grew out of the Division's program to gather information on foreign ports and a few domestic ones and to make it available to naval officers and enlisted men visiting such ports. Inquiries were directed to city officials, photographic firms, chambers of commerce, publishers, or to anyone else who could furnish the needed photographs and data. The information received was embodied in film strips and slides, with accompanying lectures, and in illustrated guidebooks. Arranged alphabetically by name of port and thereunder chronologically.

CORRESPONDENCE OF THE COMMISSION ON TRAINING CAMP ACTIVITIES. 1918-20. 2 ft. 414
Correspondence of the Commission with business firms, relating mainly to orders for equipment, merchandise, and services necessary to the work of the Commission. The copies of letters sent are from the disbursing officer responsible for paying the related accounts. Arranged alphabetically by name of firm.

CORRESPONDENCE OF ENSIGN JOSEPH LEVANSALER. 1919-21. 3 in. 415
Relates to the liaison maintained by the Social Hygiene Section with the Public Health Service, health organizations, and the medical profession; to general morale factors; to sanitation; and to other subjects. Arranged chronologically.

REPORTS FROM SHIPS AND STATIONS CONCERNING EXPENDITURES FOR RECREATION. 1920-22. 3 ft. 416
Show the status of allotments under the appropriation "Recreation for Enlisted Men" and transmit S & A Forms 51a (short), "Public Bills Afloat," for expenditures thereunder. Arranged alphabetically by name of ship or station.

Records of the Training Division, 1917-40

During World War I the administration of the program for training enlisted personnel was in charge of the Training Division of the Bureau of Navigation. The first officer at the head of this Division was Capt. Ernest L. Bennett, who reported for duty on April 19, 1917, and throughout the war superintended the huge task of providing and administering training facilities. At the opening of the war there were only four permanent training stations--at Newport, Norfolk, Great Lakes, and San Francisco--with a total capacity of 6,000 enlisted men. These stations were expanded eightfold by the erection of temporary stations or barracks on both coasts and along the Gulf of Mexico. A huge naval operating base that included a large training station was established at Hampton Roads, Va. The Training Division was also responsibile for training and instructing enlisted men who were candidates for officers' commissions. It had charge of training on naval district vessels, at special schools, and at naval rifle ranges, and of training naval units of the Students' Army Training Corps.

From 1919 to about 1923 the Division was a section in the Enlisted Personnel Division, but, according to the Secretary's Annual Report for 1923, it was again made a separate division on March 1, 1923, and was "charged with the administration of all duties relating to the training, instruction, welfare, and recreation of the personnel of the Navy and Naval Reserve Force." In it there were three sections: (1) Officers-- Training and instruction; (2) Enlisted men--Training and instruction; and (3) Welfare and Recreation. In general the training and instruction involved control of the training and school units as well as formulation of curricula, instruction, and examinations. The Welfare and Recreation Section was in charge of athletics, motion pictures, allotments to carry out its activities, libraries, and supply and disbursing. Records of the predecessor Morale Division are described in entries 410-416.

GENERAL ADMINISTRATIVE CORRESPONDENCE. 1918-23. 6 ft. 417
Concerns the relations of the Training Division with the Bureau of Navigation, other Government agencies, vessels, special schools and training units, enlisted men seeking officers' commissions, and the public. Until December 1, 1921, carbon copies of letters sent and typewritten copies of letters received were filed together and numbered serially, 1-12580.. Thereafter they are unnumbered. Arranged chronologically.

ADMINISTRATIVE CORRESPONDENCE RELATING TO TRAINING UNITS. 1917-22.
    19 ft. 418
Concerns the administration of training schools, stations, camps, and other naval training units and their appropriation allotments. Included are some inspection reports and informational material. Arranged alphabetically by subject; oversize material is separate.

CORRESPONDENCE WITH APPLICANTS FOR ADMISSION TO TRAINING SCHOOLS AND
    WITH MEN SEEKING SPECIAL RATINGS AND OFFICERS' COMMISSIONS. 1918-19.
    4 in. 419
Letters received from and copies of letters sent to navy men and civilians in answer to inquiries about training school opportunities and conditions of admission to specific schools, and to applicants for specialists' ratings and officers' commissions. Arranged alphabetically.

SYLLABUSES OF COURSES OFFERED AT NAVY TRAINING SCHOOLS. 1918-19.
3 ft.   420

These syllabuses are for all schools offering instruction under the training program of the World War I period. There is one folder for each school. The school is designated by name and by a decimal number, as "4. Cape May, N. J. -- Section Base -- Coxwains School. 4.422." Arranged by naval district and thereunder by decimal number of school. Two keys are available to these syllabuses, one showing the numbers used by the Training Division to identify each school and the other showing the naval training units and sections at educational institutions in the various States in 1918.

WEEKLY TRADE SCHOOL REPORTS. 1922-24. 2 ft.   421

Consist mainly of copies of Form N. Nav. 342, "Weekly Trade School Report," which contain, for each school, detailed information on the number of men under instruction and their ratings, the number of instructors and their ratings, the number of men in the class and the number returned to service, and similar data. In folders arranged alphabetically by location of school and thereunder alphabetically by name of school.

RECORDS OF THE WELFARE AND RECREATION SECTION. 1923-40. 7 ft.   422

Mainly correspondence relating to such subjects as athletics, motion pictures, allotments of funds, schools, ship's service activities, ship and station newspapers, welfare of naval personnel, and miscellaneous welfare activities. This series also includes correspondence relating to training camp activities, 1917-19; a small amount of correspondence of the earlier Morale and Recreation Section of the Morale Division, 1920-23, that apparently supplements the records described in entry 411; administrative, statistical, and fiscal reports; and a few manuscripts of plays. About half the correspondence is arranged according to a numeric-subject scheme under which each folder is labeled by subject and a corresponding number from 2 to 29; part of the other records are arranged by number and thereunder chronologically; and part of the records are unarranged.

REPORTS ON MORALE FACTORS AMONG ENLISTED MEN. 1924-25. 3 in.   423

These reports were submitted by the Welfare and Recreation Section of the Training Division to the Bureau of Navigation, as required by BuNav Circular Letter 91-94 of October 28, 1924. The factors rated included motion pictures, athletics, and ship or station libraries. The reports are arranged by station or division of the fleet.

REPORTS ON NAVAL RESERVE TRAINING ACTIVITIES IN MISSOURI AND INDIANA.
1923-25. 5 vols. 4 in.   424

Contain photographs, maps, statistical summaries and graphs, and typewritten narrative. Arranged by State. Two volumes contain tables of contents.

RECORDS OF OTHER ORGANIZATIONS ATTACHED TO THE BUREAU OF NAVIGATION

Records of the Signal Office, 1869-86

In 1869 the Signal Office was organized and attached to the Bureau of Navigation for the purpose of preparing signal books and codes and giving instruction in signaling. The Army method of signaling, which had proved successful during the Civil War, was introduced as an auxiliary to the Navy signal code by Brig. Gen. A. J. Myer, Chief Signal Officer of the Army and deviser of the system. Young naval officers were trained by Army signal instructors, and instruction and practice on board ships of war was introduced. Signal books were prepared for the use of the Navy and an American edition of the International Signal Code, which was used by most foreign countries and the merchant marine, was published. Because the Army method of signaling was in some respects inadequate for communications between vessels, experimentation was carried on with different types of signals such as chronosemic, phonetic, and flash signals. The Very pistol, a device for night signaling by means of red and green colored lights that was invented by Lt. Edward W. Very, USN, was introduced in 1877. After 1882 no mention is made of the Signal Office or the Chief Signal Officer in the annual reports of the Secretary of the Navy or the Chief of the Bureau of Navigation.

In addition to the records described below, letters received from the Chief Signal Officer, 1871-83, and fair copies of letters sent to the Chief Signal Officer, 1871-83, are described in entries 78 and 32, respectively.

FAIR COPIES OF LETTERS SENT ("LETTERS. NO. 1. SIGNAL OFFICE").
July 19, 1869-Jan. 16, 1882. 1 vol. 2 in. 425
This volume of fair copies duplicates in part the press copies described in entry 426. Arranged chronologically. The volume is indexed alphabetically by name of addressee.

PRESS COPIES OF LETTERS SENT. Nov. 1, 1869-Dec. 18, 1878; Jan.-Sept., 1879; and Jan. 6, 1882-Nov. 17, 1886. 4 vols. 4 in. 426
These letters, dating from the time the Signal Office was established, were sent mainly to the Bureau of Navigation, but also to the Secretary of the Navy, other Navy bureaus, and officers commanding ships, stations, and yards. They relate to routine administrative matters of the Office such as orders, instructions, and acknowledgments of reports, and to some technical signal matters. Arranged chronologically. Three of the volumes are indexed alphabetically by name of person, ship, station, yard, or subject.

Records of the Coast Signal Service, 1898

The Coast Signal Service was organized on the recommendation of a board convened by a Navy Department order dated October 18, 1897. Pursuant to orders of the Secretary of the Navy of March 15, 1898, Capt. Caspar F. Goodrich, president of the Naval War College, reported a plan for the establishment of coast signal stations on the Atlantic and Gulf coasts, based on the board's recommendation. On April 9, 1898, only a few days before war with Spain was declared, Captain Goodrich was ordered to establish these stations. He located his headquarters in New York and on April 22 telegraphed the commanding officers of the Naval Militia of the seaboard States to establish and man the coast signal stations already decided on. On May 9 Capt. John R. Bartlett, chief intelligence officer, was placed in command of the Service. He moved the headquarters to Washington, where it operated under the supervision of the Bureau of Navigation. Eight districts were created in which 36 signal stations were maintained by State Naval Militia. The Life Saving Service, the Lighthouse Service, and the Weather Bureau cooperated with the Coast Signal Service in maintaining a lookout for the approach of enemy vessels and in checking the movements of American vessels. The Service was discontinued at the close of the Spanish-American War.

CORRESPONDENCE REGARDING THE ESTABLISHMENT OF SIGNAL STATIONS. Mar. 15-Apr. 21, 1898. 1 vol. 3 in. 427

Letters and telegrams received and press copies of letters sent by the headquarters of the Service. The correspondence, some of which is marked "confidential," is mainly with the Navy Department and with naval officers stationed outside Washington. Included are orders to Capt. Caspar F. Goodrich. The letters relate to the best methods of signaling and to pertinent technical and scientific matters, to types of signal structures (with drawings, blueprints, and a few photographs), to offers of service from State Naval Militia and from individuals, and to business and housekeeping matters. Arranged chronologically.

HEADQUARTERS CORRESPONDENCE WITH NAVY BUREAUS AND GOVERNMENT DEPARTMENTS. Apr. 22-Sept. 20, 1898. 1 vol. 3 in. 428

Contains letters, telegrams, and endorsements received and sent by the headquarters of the Service, including some orders to signal stations. The records relate to the organization, administration, financing, supply, manning, and operation of the Service. Arranged chronologically.

CORRESPONDENCE OF DISTRICT HEADQUARTERS WITH SIGNAL STATIONS. Apr.-Aug. 1898. 2 vols. 8 in. 429

Letters, telegrams, and endorsements exchanged between district headquarters and signal stations. They concern routine reporting, personnel, business, and administrative matters and include orders from district headquarters to the stations. Arranged by number of district, thereunder by station, and thereunder chronologically. Correspondence of the Fifth District is missing; some of it may be bound with the correspondence described in entry 438.

CORRESPONDENCE WITH THE FIRST DISTRICT OFFICE AT BOSTON, MASS. Apr. 22-Aug. 17, 1898. 1 vol. 3 in. 430

Letters, telegrams, and endorsements exchanged mainly between the

Headquarters Office and the First District Office, concerning routine business and administrative matters of the district office and the stations under its control. The First District (or Division) comprised stations at Bakers Island, Vinalhaven, Cape Elizabeth, Appledore Island, Cape Ann, Cape Cod, and Gay Head. Arranged chronologically.

LETTERS SENT BY THE COMMANDING OFFICER OF THE FIRST DISTRICT ("LETTERS"). Apr. 22-Aug. 7, 1898. 2 vols. 3 in.   431

Press copies of letters and telegrams sent to the Headquarters Office, to signal stations in the First District, to bureaus of the Navy Department, to navy yards, and to business firms. They relate mainly to routine reporting of ships sighted, procurement of signal equipment and other supplies, and low-echelon administrative, personnel, and "housekeeping" affairs. There are also copies of orders. Arranged chronologically. The volumes are indexed alphabetically by name of addressee.

CORRESPONDENCE WITH THE SECOND DISTRICT OFFICE AT NEW YORK. Apr. 24-Sept. 28, 1898. 1 vol. 3 in.   432

The correspondence in this series is similar to that described in entry 430. The Second District (or Division) comprised stations at Block Island, Montauk Point, Fire Island, Quogue, Barnegat, and Cape Henlopen. Arranged chronologically.

MISCELLANEOUS LETTERS SENT BY HEADQUARTERS OF THE SECOND DISTRICT. Apr. 29-June 30, 1898. 1 vol. 1 in.   433

Press copies of miscellaneous letters sent. Arranged chronologically. Indexed alphabetically by subject, name, or station.

LETTERS SENT BY HEADQUARTERS OF THE SECOND DISTRICT TO STATIONS ("STATIONS"). June 24-Aug. 8, 1898. 1 vol. 1 in.   434

Press copies of letters and orders sent from the headquarters of the Second District at New York, concerning station business such as authorizations to purchase supplies and equipment, routine administration, personnel actions, inspections, and submission of forms and reports. Arranged chronologically. Indexed by station and thereunder chronologically.

LETTERS SENT BY THE COMMANDING OFFICER OF THE SECOND DISTRICT TO THE HEADQUARTERS OFFICE ("HEADQUARTERS"). June 24-Aug. 14, 1898. 1 vol. 1 in.   435

Press copies of letters and telegrams sent to the Superintendent of the Service. They concern routine reporting, administration, supply, and personnel matters. Arranged chronologically. Indexed alphabetically by subject, name, or place.

CORRESPONDENCE WITH THE THIRD DISTRICT OFFICE AT NORFOLK, VA. Apr. 22-Aug. 15, 1898. 1 vol. 3 in.   436

The correspondence in this series is similar to that described in entry 430. The Third District (or Division) comprised stations at Cape Henry, Hatteras Inlet, Cape Lookout, and Carolina Beach. Arranged chronologically.

CORRESPONDENCE WITH THE FOURTH DISTRICT OFFICE AT CHARLESTON, S. C. Apr. 23-Sept. 11, 1898. 1 vol. 3 in.   437

The correspondence in this series is similar to that described in entry 430. The Fourth District (or Division) comprised stations at Charleston (Morris Island), Hiltonhead Island, Tybee Island, and St. Simon Island. Arranged chronologically.

CORRESPONDENCE WITH THE FIFTH DISTRICT OFFICE AT JACKSONVILLE, FLA. Apr. 22-Sept. 17, 1898. 1 vol. 2 in.   438

The correspondence in this series is similar to that described in entry 430. The Fifth District (or Division) comprised stations on the St. Johns River and at Cape Canaveral, Jupiter Inlet, and Miami. Arranged chronologically.

CORRESPONDENCE WITH THE SIXTH DISTRICT OFFICE AT PENSACOLA, FLA. Apr. 22-Aug. 29, 1898. 1 vol. 3 in.   439

The correspondence in this series is similar to that described in entry 430. The Sixth District (or Division) comprised stations at the Pensacola Navy Yard and on Santa Rosa Island. Arranged chronologically.

CORRESPONDENCE WITH THE SEVENTH DISTRICT OFFICE AT NEW ORLEANS, LA. Apr. 23-Sept. 19, 1898. 1 vol. 2 in.   440

The correspondence in this series is similar to that described in entry 430. The Seventh District (or Division) comprised stations at Fort Morgan, Port Eads, and Galveston. Arranged chronologically.

TELEGRAMS RELATING TO MOVEMENTS OF VESSELS. Apr.-Aug. 1898. 1 vol. 4 in.   441

These are both originals and copies of telegrams received and sent by the headquarters of the Service, by district headquarters, and by stations. Arranged by district reporting, thereunder either unarranged or arranged in part by station, and thereunder in general chronologically.

Records of the Board of Visitors of the Naval Academy, 1910-13

In 1851 a Board of Visitors was appointed by the President to attend the annual examinations at the Academy and to report on the condition of the school. This Board has customarily been composed of high-ranking naval officers and civilians and its annual report is submitted to the President of the United States. The Board looks into the state of discipline and the general management of the Academy and makes recommendations for such changes and improvements as it sees fit. During the period covered by the following records the Academy was under the Bureau of Navigation. Records of other boards drawing part of their membership from the Bureau of Navigation are described in the <u>Checklist of the Naval Records Collection</u> and in the <u>Checklist of the General Records of the Department of the Navy, 1804-1944</u>.

JACKETS OF APPOINTEES TO AND APPLICANTS FOR MEMBERSHIP ON THE BOARD OF VISITORS OF THE NAVAL ACADEMY. 1910-13. 10 in. 442

These jackets (Form N. Nav. 153) contain mainly applications of and recommendations for both successful and unsuccessful applicants for membership on the Board, together with acceptances, notices of appointment, and other material relating to appointments. The series also includes some loose papers such as lists of appointees and Presidential correspondence. Arranged in two groups, one for successful applicants (labeled "Board of Visitors, 1911") and one for unsuccessful applicants.

RECORDS OF UNITS OF THE BUREAU OF NAVAL PERSONNEL AND OF THE NAVAL RESEARCH PERSONNEL BOARD, 1940-46

The change from Bureau of Navigation to Bureau of Naval Personnel in May 1942 was a change of name and organization rather than a change of functions. After the transfer in April 1942 of the Hydrographic Office and the Naval Observatory to the Office of the Chief of Naval Operations, only personnel functions remained for the Bureau of Navigation. Many series of records--particularly correspondence, logs, and muster rolls--were continued on without a break by the new Bureau; they have already been described under the heading "General Records of the Bureau of Naval Personnel." Most of the records described below are those created by units of the Bureau that came into existence after May 1942 and that maintained separate series of records.

Records of the Planning and Control Activity, n.d.

ADMINISTRATIVE HISTORY OF THE BUREAU OF NAVAL PERSONNEL IN WORLD WAR II. n.d. 15 vols. 1 ft. 443

Copies of separate reports on each of the important activities of the Bureau having to do with officer, enlisted, and civilian personnel of the Navy Department, including reports on the Structural Development of BuPers, Planning and Control Activity, Officer Personnel Activity, Training Activity, Welfare Activity, and Enlisted Personnel Activity. There are also separate reports on phases of the work of each activity as, for example, Enlisted Performance, Chaplain's Division, Officer Distribution, and Women's Reserve. Arranged by activity, thereunder by volume number or phase of work. Each volume is indexed according to the organization of the report.

Records of the Office of the Chief of Naval Personnel, 1942-45

REGULATIONS GOVERNING WOMEN ACCEPTED FOR VOLUNTEER EMERGENCY SERVICE. July 1942-Nov. 1945. 2 vols. 2 in. 444

This "record set" of regulations consists of two volumes labeled as follows: (1) "NavPers-15,085 (Restricted), 'Policies for the Administration of the Women's Reserve, United States Naval Reserve'" and (2) "References in 'Policies for the Administration of the Women's Reserve, USNR.'" The first volume consists of printed material; the second, of typewritten and processed material. Both volumes are indexed, the first by title of article and the second by subject and thereunder by title of article, circular, letter, and the like.

Records of the Special Services Division of the Welfare Activity, 1942-46

GENERAL RECORDS OF THE PHYSICAL FITNESS SECTION. 1942-46. 34 ft. 445

Relate to the inception, organization, and administration of the Navy's physical fitness program during World War II. The records include applications for appointments, together with supporting papers; personal correspondence and orders of officers; correspondence and propaganda material designed to get famous athletes to participate in the Navy physical training program; and other material concerning different phases of the program. Arranged mainly according to the classification scheme of the Navy Filing Manual.

GENERAL RECORDS OF THE RECREATIONAL SERVICES SECTION. 1943-46. 30 ft. 446

These records are a basic source of information on the inception, organization, administration, and activities of the United Service Organization's units operating under naval jurisdiction. The series includes some personnel records, mainly correspondence relating to civilian and service personnel. Most of the records in this series are arranged according to a subject-numeric classification scheme from 1 (American Red Cross) through 65 (Women's Reserve Division). Copies of the classification scheme are available. The correspondence relating to civilian and service personnel is arranged alphabetically by name of person.

Records of the Recruiting and Induction Division, 1940-45

RECORDS OF THE PUBLICITY AND ADVERTISING SECTION RELATING TO THE NAVY RECRUITING PROGRAM. 1940-45. 4 ft. 447

Include scrapbooks containing comic strips and newspaper clippings, classified by subject to show the advantages of Navy service. These books have a table of contents on the cover. Other binders contain clippings relating to some branch of the Navy, as the Seabees, the Waves, and the Ship Repair Units. The series also includes enlistment posters and display bulletins that emphasize the advantages and duties of persons already in the Navy; two copies of a Navy "Handbook for Procurement Personnel"; and a booklet of photographs of displays of Wave enlistment posters in show windows of a power company office and its branch offices (May and June 1943). Except that two types of scrapbooks and posters are filed in groups, the records are unarranged.

Records of the Naval Research Personnel Board, 1944-45

The Naval Research Personnel Board was convened by the Secretary of the Navy in March 1944 to facilitate the militarization of civilian specialists employed in certain laboratories and other technical establishments of the Navy so that the services of these specialists would not be lost by their induction into the armed forces. Records of other boards drawing part or all of their membership from the Bureau of Navigation are described in the Checklist of the Naval Records Collection and in the Checklist of the General Records of the Department of the Navy, 1804-1944.

GENERAL RECORDS OF THE BOARD. Mar. 1944-Sept. 19, 1945. 2 ft. 448
Relate to the basic policies, procedures, and decisions of the Board. The series includes general correspondence, investigative and other reports from such agencies as the War Manpower Commission and the Civil Service Commission, notices of induction into the Naval Reserve, requests for increase in complement of personnel, and minutes of the Board's meetings. A few items are marked "confidential." Unarranged.

APPENDIX

PARTIAL SUBJECT INDEX TO THE GENERAL CORRESPONDENCE OF THE BUREAU OF NAVIGATION, 1903-25

These subjects, selected from a much larger total number, are from the numerical-record cards described in entry 92. The number or numbers following the subject are those under which the correspondence for this period was filed; bracketed notations are those supplied by the author and are not on the cards.

Abyssinia, 4143
Accidents, 2295; aviation, 57360-4
Addressographs, 7811
Admiral of the Navy, Secretary to, 6024
Advertising, 684, 6071
Aero Club bulletins, 9356
Aeronautics, Bureau of, 57236, 57252
Agents on ships, 5838
Agriculture, Department of, 6008
Airships, 5901
Airships and seaplanes (aviation), 57360-6
Air stations at
  Akron, Ohio, 20789
  Anacostia, D. C., 27116
  Bay Shore, Long Island, N. Y., 17673
  Brunswick, Ga., 50812
  Chatham, Mass., 30462
  Halifax, Nova Scotia, 40691
  Miami, Fla., 14228
  Montauk, Long Island, N. Y., 24285
  Moorehead City, N. C., 46033
  North Sydney, Nova Scotia, 40690
  Pensacola, Fla., 9321
  Rockaway, Long Island, N. Y., 22627
  San Diego (North Island), Calif., 20635
  Squantum, Mass., 15079
  Toronto, Canada, 22490
Alaska, 2479
Allotments, 2383
Allowance books, 7198

Allowances, 7300; money, 7377
Ammunition, 2849
Amusements, 2807
Anchorages, 524, 5648
Anniversary exercises, 2366
Annual report, 2217
Applications
  In general, 3422, 4048
  Assistant paymasters, 7259
  Carpenters, 529, 5524
  Collier officers, 668
  Commissioned officers, 2769
  Enlistment, 1920, 5705, 57358-03
  Naval Auxiliary Service, 7368
  Paymaster's clerks, 7260
  Professors of mathematics, 609
Appointments, 3157
Apprentices, 2405
Appropriations, 1993, 9468, 57372; transfer of hospital, 1027
  Gunnery examination and engineering performance, 57372-05
  Instruments and supplies, 57372-03
  Naval Reserve, 57372-02
  Ocean and lake survey, 57372-04
  Stations, 57372-06
  Transportation and recruiting, 57372-01
Armed guard, 10571
Armor plant, Government, 8551
Army and Navy Medal of Honor Roll, 9701
Army General Orders, 3088, 5561
Army Reserve, 10227
Asiatic events, report of, 673
Assistance, offers of, 10072
Associations, 2779

Attachés, visits of, 6156, 923
Auditor for the Navy Department, 1995
Automobile trucks, 12438
Automobiles, 6253
Auxiliary Naval Force, Fourth District (Spanish War), 5281
Aviation, general, 57360; balloons, 57360-2; training, 57360-3
Aviators, civilian, 9870

Badges:
  Dominican Campaign, 55915
  Haitian Campaign, 9532
  Mexican Campaign, 8935
  Nicaraguan Campaign, 8565
Baggage, 4971
Bands, 512, 2125
Barracks, 3389
Bases
  Advance, 5271
  Destroyer Base at San Diego, Calif., 57381
  Fleet Supply Base
    Brooklyn, N. Y., 37784
    San Diego, Calif., 56682
  Naval Operating Base
    General, 43063
    Appropriations, 43063-05
    Canal Zone, 57233
    Complements, 43063-04
    Estimates, 43063-06
    Hampton Roads, Va., 19270
    Key West, Fla., 57234
    Requisitions, 43063-02
    Schedules and contracts, 43063-01
    Schools, 43063-03
  Submarine Base
    Coco Solo, C. Z., 28837
    New London, Conn., 9531
Beneficiaries, 6191
Bills of Exchange, 2299
Biograph Pictures, 5287
Blanks, 2826
Bluejacket, 6480
Boards: general, 3843, 57366; examining, 872, 6756; mooring, 6234; retiring, 1303

Boards (continued)
  Board of Inspection and Survey, 4356
  Board of Visitors, Naval Academy, 927
  Board on Awards, 4529
  Board on Awards in Competitive Target Firing, 2865
  Board on Construction, 3151
  Board on Larchmont Collision, 1723
  Chart Board, 2162
  Federal Specification Board, 57325
  General Board, 1818
  Interdepartmental Board on Boundaries and Privileges, 5829
  Light House Board, 6013
  Review Board, 56093
  Selection Board, 9893
Boat landings, 4357
Boats, 2134
Boatswain, acting, examinations for, 2843
Boatswain Hill Trust Fund, 9553
Bonuses, 50302
Books, 2925
Brass and copper pipes, 6343
Brass melting furnaces (on board ship), 7067
Brazilian Naval Mission, 57885
Budget system, 57225
Buenos Aires Expositions, 6995
Buildings, 4322
Buoys, 2690

Cadets' quarters building, 1129
Calendars, 901
Canals, 3743
Canteens, 5163
Card index, 2161
Carriage hire, 2943
Carrier pigeons, 31118
Casualties, 573
Celebrations, 1025, 5562
Censorship, 9559
Census, 7069

Certificates of qualification, 6124
Chaplains, 526, 5732
Charts, 912
Chemical warfare, 36874
Chile, 4065
China, 3142
Chronometers, 7132
Circular letters, 1020
Citizenship, 3181
Civil courts, 6122
Civil engineers, 1374
Civil Service Commission, 1681, 6052
Claims, 2691; for pay, 2066
Clothing, 2860
Clubs, 5742
Coal, 528, 5559
Coal barges, 1822, 3206
Coaling, 4359
Coaling ships, 681
Coast and Geodetic Survey, 8573
Coast defense, 1657
Coast Defense Reserve, 9878
Coast Guard, 8908
Colleges, 3891
Colliers, 1569
 Commanding officers, 615
 Crews, 527, 5710; pay of, 2196
 Regulations, 1092
Columbia University [training in engineering], 29909
Commendations, 5306
Commerce, Department of, 8905
Commerce and Labor, Department of, 6168
Committee on Training Camp Activities
 American Library Association, 55401
 American Red Cross, 55399
 American Social Hygiene Association, 55406
 Athletics, 55409
 Entertainments, 55408
 Jewish Welfare Board, 55405
 Law enforcement, 55414
 Lectures re morals, 55413

Committee on Training Camp Activities (continued)
 Libraries, 55415
 Motion pictures, 55407
 Music, 55410
 National War Council, 55402
 Organization and establishment, 55412
 Policy, 55411
 Recreational equipment, 55417
 Salvation Army, 55419
 Song leaders, 55416
 War camp community service, 55418
 YMCA, 55403
Compass reports, 57359-02
Compasses, 5778, 57359
Complaints, 2480, 3328
Concrete construction, 4046
Confidential Bulletin, 2154
Congress (Senate), 1385
Congresses, 2710
Construction and Repair, Bureau of, 2316
Construction Corps, 7366
Consuls, U. S., 1996
Contracts, 619
Coppersmiths, 6860
Correspondents, 2310
Courts
 Civil, 6122
 Court of Claims, 5780
 Court of Inquiry, 4546
Courts martial, 637, 5554, 57367
Cuba, 833, 3969
Curaçao, West Indies, affairs of, 2972
Customs, 7073

Deaths, 4457
Debts, 584, 4865, 8340, 57357
Decisions, 702
Dentists, 2768
Deposits, 5774
Depots and magazines
 Bradford, R. I., Naval Coal Depot, 5154

Depots and magazines (continued)
  California City Point Coal Depot, 6121
  Cañacao, P. I., Medical Supply Depot, 6267
  Frenchman Bay Coaling Depot, 3719
  Lake Denmark, N. J., Naval Powder Depot, 6078
  Naval magazines, 2920
Deserters, 759, 918, 57375
Designations (aviation), 57360-5
Despatch agent, London, 7068
Destroyers (1914), 8111
Diplomats, 796
Discharges, 1120, 57364
Discourtesies, 2016
Divers and diving, 7470
Docking, 3562; foreign ports, 3027
Docks, 2990
Drafts, 3091
Drawings, 2999
Drills and evolutions, 1527
Dry Tortugas, 3339
Dunwoody Institute, 20950
Dutch ships, 30689

Eagle boats, general, 30471
Earthquakes, 4568; Italy, 6392
Economic Liaison Committee, 56619
Effects, 2704
Electricians, 2836
Ellis Island, 6090
Employees, miscellaneous, 6344
Employers, miscellaneous, 752
Engineers: civil, 1374; civilian, 9783
Enlisted men
  Efficiency of, on recruiting duty, 6972
  Pay of, 562, 5570
  Records for, 5787
Enlistments, 525, 5525, 57358
  Circulars, 598, 57358-01
  Records of, 2019
  Reports of, 57358-02
Epidemic, 589

Equipment, Bureau of, 3634
Equipment of ships, 2127
Estimates, 1677, 3696
European conditions, 1808
European Detachment, nominations of officers for, 57314
European War, 8768
Executive orders, 5309
Expeditions, 1090
Experimental and Research Laboratory, Bellevue, D. C., 58358
Explosions, 2814
Expositions, 1590

Fish Commission, U. S., 1848
Fish nets, 5147
Flagpole, 5826
Flags, 1308
Fleet and squadron regulations, 6007
Fleet Base Force
  General, 57895
  Aircraft squadrons, 57895-03
  Destroyer squadrons, 57895-02
  Mine squadrons, 57895-01
  Training, 57895-04
Fleet Naval Reserve, 9872
[Fleets, squadrons, and subdivisions thereof]
  [Asiatic]
    Fleet, 6581, 57886
      Enlisted personnel, 57886-02
      General Orders and Circulars, 672, 7060
      Officers, 57886-01; nominations of, 57312
      Orders issued to officers by despatch (incoming), 57224
      Target practice, 2231
    Station, 904, 2745, 5690
  [Atlantic]
    Fleet, 6072, 57361
      Air Force, nominations of officers, 57310-04
      Battleship Force, nominations of officers, 57310

[Fleets, squadrons, and subdivisions thereof] (continued)
  [Atlantic] (continued)
    Fleet (continued)
      Control Force, nominations of officers, 57310-06
      Destroyer Force, nominations of officers, 57310-01
      General Orders and Circulars, 6150; Atlantic Training Squadron, 4150
      Mine Force, nominations of officers, 57310-05
      Orders issued to officers by despatch (incoming), 57222
      Sixth Division, 5268
      Submarine divisions
        General, 57889
        Enlisted personnel, 57889-02
        Officers, 57889-01
      Submarine Force, nominations of officers, 57310-02
      Third Squadron, 6280
      Third Submarine Division, 7025
      Training Force, nominations of officers, 57310-03
    Reserve Fleet, 7766
    Training Squadron, 3791
    Battle Fleet
      General, 57892
      Aircraft squadrons, 57892-04
      Battleship divisions, 57892-01
      Destroyer squadrons, 57892-03
      Submarine divisions, 57892-05
    Battleship Squadron movements, 1956
    Control Force
      General, 57894
      Cruiser divisions, 57894-01
      Destroyer squadrons, 59894-02
      Mine squadrons, 57894-03
  Eleventh Fleet, 6193
  [European]
    Naval Forces
      General, 57887

[Fleets, squadrons, and subdivisions thereof] (continued)
  [European] (continued)
    Naval Forces (continued)
      Enlisted personnel, 57887-02
      Officers, 57887-01
    Squadron
      Movements, 2394
      Target practice, 2229
    Station, 1528, 2081
  Midshipmen's Practice Squadron, 5837
  Nicaraguan Expeditionary Squadron, 6880
  [North Atlantic]
    Fleet
      Caribbean Division, 2098, 3349
      Coast Squadron, 2828, 3514
      Fourth Division, Second Squadron, 5184
      General Orders and Circulars, 753
      Third Squadron, 5183
    Station, 1754
  [Pacific]
    Coast, squadron for, 5902
    Fleet, 5690, 57363
      Air Force, nominations of officers, 57311-04
      Battleship Force, nominations of officers, 57311
      Destroyer Force, nominations of officers, 57311-01
      General Orders and Circulars, 6192
      Mine Force, nominations of officers, 57311-05
      Orders issued to officers by despatch (incoming), 57223
      Submarine Force, nominations of officers, 57311-02
      Training Force, nominations of officers, 57311-03
    Reserve Fleet, 7552
    Squadron, 2107; movements, 2294

[Fleets, squadrons, and subdivisions thereof] (continued)
  [Pacific] (continued)
    Station
      Squadron General Orders and Circulars, 2152
      Target practice, 2223
    Submarine divisions
      General, 57890
      Enlisted personnel, 57890-02
      Officers, 57890-01
  Reserve Battleship Fleet, 6877
  Scouting Fleet
    General, 57893
    Aircraft squadron, 57893-04
    Battleship divisions, 57893-01
    Destroyer squadrons, 57893-03
    Light cruiser divisions, 57893-02
    Submarine divisions, 57893-05
    Training, 57893-06
  [South Atlantic]
    Squadron
      General, 869
      Complement, 3718
      Target practice, 2230
    Station
      General Orders and Circulars, 2298
  [Special Service Squadron]
    General, 5151, 5831, 5979, 6169, 8036, 57888
    Enlisted personnel, 57888-02
    Officers, 57888-01; nominations of, 57313
  [U. S. Fleet]
    General, 57896
    Enlisted personnel, 57896-02
    Officers, 57896-01
Flood in Ohio Valley, 8403
Flotillas
  Atlantic Submarine, 9338
  First Submarine, 5743
  First Torpedo, 3035; miscellaneous, 3086
  Fourth Torpedo Boat, 6154
  Reserve Torpedo, 2869
  Second Submarine, 4272

Flotillas (continued)
  Second Torpedo, 2974
  Third Torpedo, 5162
  Torpedo, 1241, 5177
  Torpedo, Atlantic, 6634
  Torpedo, movements, 935
Flying Corps Naval Reserve, 9879
Fort Mifflin, Pa., 6005
Fourth Naval Defense District, 3975
Free entry, 1387
Fuel, 3466
  Federal distribution, 35285
  Ships (1913), 7943
Funerals, 2175
Furniture, 2904

Gas and gasoline engines, 6157
Gas masks, 24546
Gasoline and liquid fuel, 3877
General Order No. 13 (Feb. 24, 1909), 6574
General Orders, 4713
Geographic names, 5297
German chargé d'affaires, 6272
German spies, 9149
Graves, 4311
Greece, 6764
Guadeloupe, West Indies, 5391
Guam, 1077
Guantánamo, Cuba, 6159
Guatemala, 5426
Gulf of St. Lawrence, 5862
Gun pointers, 3971
Gunner, acting, 2530
Gunnery instructions, 4056
Guns, condemned, 4066

Habeas corpus cases, 1582
Haiti, 868
Haiti and Santo Domingo, condition of affairs in, 2755
Harbors, 1875
Helium plant, Texas, 54126
History, 4227
Honduras affairs, 1967
Honorable discharge blanks, 57364-01

Hospital Corps, 2157, 3982
Hospital ship (1915), 8151
Hospital ships, 1810
Hospitals, 2135, 2702; medical equipment, 5398; transfer of appropriations, 1027
Hotels, 6091
Houses, portable, 5275
Hydrographic information, 638, 5785
Hydrographic Office, 6914; branch offices, 3302, 6550
Hydrographic surveys, 638

Identification, 5397
Identification tags, 8574
Imposters, 6341
Income tax, 8562
Indian Head, Md., 4963
Insane, 5167
Inspections, 5127
Inspectors, 3783, 6074
Instruction of young officers, 6086
Instructions, 1024
Instruments, aviation, 57360-1
Insular possessions, 2046
Intelligence outfits, 3697
Interior, Department of, 1414
International fencing class in Rome, 6793
Inventions, 2264
Isthmus of Panama, affairs in, 2221

Japan, 5912; condition of affairs in, 4436
Japanese Exposition, 6274
Judge Advocate General, Office of the, 6112

Landing forces, 8580
Landing foreign troops, 5841
Lands, 2862
Languages, foreign, 6092
Leaves, 794
Lectures, 4136
Legations, 5146

Legislation, 1864, 4494, 57368
Letters of introduction, 3426
Liability Act, 6273
Liberia, 5199; Commission, 6632
Libraries, ships, 2835
Lighthouses, 3104
Log books, 659, 5269
Longitudes, establishment of, 3996
Long-range spotting, 6252

Machinery, 2205
Mail: Private, 723, 5534; official, 595, 5538
Maintenance of ships in commission, 6239
Maneuvers: Culebra, 568; summer, 2250; winter, 3755
Marine band, 8582
Marine Corps, 1661; discharges, 8583
Marines, 942
Massachusetts Institute of Technology, 24292
Master's license, 6423
Mates, 3353
Medals, 1662; campaign, 6246; victory, 54688; West Indies, 1171, 2076
Medals of honor, 1474
Medical equipment, hospital ships, 5398
Medical Reserve Corps, 7294
Medicine and Surgery, Bureau of, 1131
Men available, 5953
Men ordered to Europe, 15205
Merchant Marine, 16655
Merchant vessels, 40949
Messmen, 5325
Metal polishes, 6424
Mexico, 1646
Midshipmen, 591; notification to Congressmen, 2516; reports of fitness of, 5145
Midway Islands, 1581
Mine and mine sweeping divisions, 9361
Mine sweepers, 15401

Miscellaneous, 2915
[Miscellaneous stations]
  Alexandria, Va., Torpedo Station, 45597
  Arlington, Va., Radio Station, 8040
  Coaling stations, 857
  Lakehurst, N. J., Experiment Station, 45344
  Life saving stations, 5744
  Long Island, N. Y., Torpedo Testing Station, 7207
  Manila, P. I., proposed torpedo station at, 6748
  Newport, R. I., Torpedo Station, 2820
  Pacific coast, proposed torpedo station on, 6209
  San Diego, Calif., Coaling Station, 6163
  Shore stations, 6326
Mississippi River, 2973
Mississippi tornado, 6171
Mobilization plans, 9363
Models, 5144
Money, 2996
Money allowances, 7377
Money orders, 6004
Monthly address book, 6213
Monuments, 2207
Motor Boat Corps, 9346
Music, 2300
Musicians, 5781
Muster rolls, 1494

Nautical Almanac, 6749, 7131
Nautical schools, 1052
[Naval Academy]
  General, 1579, 1704, 3983, 6073
  Appropriations, 39831-04
  Artesian well, 755
  Athletics, 39831-06
  Board of Visitors correspondence, 927
  Boathouse, 2047
  Chapel, 3543
  Complement, 39831-03
  Contracts and schedules, 39831 01

[Naval Academy] (continued)
  Dredging, 2588
  Estimates, 39831-05
  General improvements, 2338
  Gymnasium, 506
  Lands, 1803
  Marine barracks at, 2793
  Marine Engineering and Construction Building, 2354
  Mess quarters for officers, 507
  Officers' quarters, 500
  Paving, 2641
  Postgraduate school, 39831-07
  Powerhouse, 502
  Powerplant, 503
  Progress of work, 882
  Proposed Naval Academy, 9779
  Publications, 7491
  Requisitions, 39831-02
  Seawall, 501
  Stable, 3753
  Superintendent's house, 3659
Naval attachés, 2850; London, 1655; Rome, 6861
Naval Auxiliary Reserve, 9876
[Naval bases and operating bases]
  Bermuda Naval Base, 28838
  San Francisco Naval Operating Base, 29281
  San Pedro, Calif.; Submarine Base, 17653
Naval battery, 30355
[Naval Districts]
  First District, Naval Patrol, 3769
  Second District, 592, 12053
  Third District, 10525
  Fourth District, 3975
  Fifth District, 3507
  Sixth District, 3508
  Seventh District, 4298
  Eighth District, 4026
  Ninth, Tenth, and Eleventh Districts, 11174
  Eleventh District, 11196
  Twelfth District, 793
  Thirteenth District, 11892
  Fourteenth District, 12664

[Naval Districts] (continued)
  Fifteenth District, 24845
  Sixteenth District, 50692
  Gulf Naval District, 3516
  Pacific Naval District, 793
Naval Gun Factory, 2839
[Naval Home, Philadelphia]
  General, 1133, 57905
  Appropriations, 57905-05
  Complement, 57905-04
  Contracts and schedules, 57905-01
  Estimates, 57905-06
  Requisitions, 57905-02
Naval Militia
  Permits for examinations, 9353
  Ships, 2241, 2469
[Naval Militias of States and Territories]
  Calif., 3325
  Conn., 3603
  Colo., 3084
  Fla., 7424
  Ga., 2867
  Ill., 3647
  La., 5155
  Maine, 3713
  Md., 3504
  Mass., 2830
  Mich., 3434
  Minn., 4700
  Mo., 4874
  N. C., 3756
  N. J., 3004
  N. Y., 4062
  Ohio, 3552
  Oreg., 7324
  Pa., 3244
  R. I., 4968
  S. C., 5381
  Tex., 9150
  T. H., 9558
  Va., 9486
  Wash., 6120
Naval Observatory, 1327, 2014
Naval Ordnance Plant, Charleston, W. Va., 49188
Naval Overseas Transportation Service, 46214

Naval personnel, disposition of, 9358
Naval Reserve, 3911, 6757, 9875
  Legislation, 7182
  Monthly report of officers enrolled, 10413
  Volunteer, 9877
[Naval Stations]
  Cavite, P. I., 620, 2317; complement, 4380
  Culebra, P. R., 1452
  Havana, Cuba, 590
  Honolulu, T. H., 936
  Key West, Fla., 3199; complement, 3509
  Narragansett Bay, R. I., 6362
  New Orleans, La., 4068
  Newport, R. I.
    Auditorium, 2000
    Officers' quarters, 3309
  Port Royal, S. C., 3078
  Puerto Rico, 941
  Tutuila, Samoa, 1738; complement, 798
Naval Supply Fund, 7077
[Naval training schools, camps, etc.]
  Cooks, bakers, and commissary stewards, school for, 5957
  Electricity, school of, 6730
  Enlisted schools, quarterly reports of, 8828
  Experimental summer schools at Great Lakes and Hampton Roads, 56986
  Fuel oil school, 34087
  Machinists' school, 7208
  Marine Engineering Design School, 6720
  Nautical School at Puget Sound, 6012
  Naval training camps
    Detroit, Mich., 36427
    San Diego, Calif., **16664**
  Officer-Material School for Pay Corps at Princeton University, 40692

[Naval training schools, camps, etc.] (continued)
  Naval Training Unit at Yale University, 23514
  Optical Mechanics' School at Washington, D. C., 31115
  Petty officers' schools, 1276
  Radio School at Harvard University, 22291
[Naval Training Stations]
  Great Lakes, Ill., 1965, 54519
    Appropriations, 54519-05
    Buildings and grounds, 5382
    Complement, 7311, 54519-04
    Estimates, 54519-06
    Requisitions, 54519-02
    Schedules and contracts, 54519-01
    Schools, 54519-03
  Gulfport, Miss., 22015
  Newport, R. I., 982, 2515, 6075, 16456; complement, 2841
  San Francisco, Calif., 563, 1962, 5549, 11086
  Training stations, 4111
Naval War College, 2183
Navigating instruments, 5790, 7158
[Navigation, Bureau of]
  Criticisms of, 6066
  Employees of, 720, 57373
  Manual, 31847
  News bulletin, 57881
  Orders, 504
  Work of, 1211
Navy, 5814
  Cookbook, 6287
  Department library, 3179
  League, 3209, 4343
  Mail clerks, 6216
  Organization, 1159, 57365
  Pay, 24447
  Pay officers, 2445, 4360
  Regulations, 963; requests for, 611
  Relief Society, 4333
  Store, 5864
Nicaragua, 5051
Nimrod Sound, 548

Nurses, 4778, 8418

Obstructions, 2675
Officers: duties of, 3031; foreign, 3903; orders to, 6194; pay of, 881; physical tests for, 6356; reserve, 9354; retired, 6352; temporary, Regular Navy, 15372
Oil, 5553, 9362
Oil burners, 6089
Olongapo, P. I., 2145
Opium, 5242
Ordnance, 2211
Ordnance, Bureau of, 5225
Orinoco River, 5176
Outfits, 1882

Paint and painting, 5543
Paintings, 5836
Panama Canal, 4545
Paper, 6318
Passengers, 518, 5255, 24000; requests of, for passage, 24027
Patriotic societies, 7072
Pay clerks, 1856
Paymasters, assistant, 1660
Peace Commission, 5137
Pensions, 1869
Permits for examination, Naval Militia, 9353
Personal expense, 4452
[Personnel, Naval Auxiliary Service], 8419
Pharmacist, 6085
Philippine mails, 5811
Philippines, 956; war in, 3906
Photographs, 1071
Pigeons, carrier, 31118
Pilots and pilotage, 1134
Plotting device, 6351
Posters, 4955, 5704
Postgraduate course, 8039
Post office boxes, 6288
Power plants, 6123
Presentations to persons, 1098
Presentations to persons and ships, 57353
Printing, 701, 57374
Printing outfits, 7378

Prisoners, 1464
Prizes, 2712
Promotions, 871
Proposed repair ship complements, 6857
Publications, 530, 5270, 57371
Pullman accommodations, 618
Punishment, 3711

Quarantine, 1487
Quarters, 5571

Rank and precedence, 2108
Ratings, 2158
Rations, 772
[Receiving ships]
  General, 8433
  Boston, 7701
  Brooklyn, 7763
  Mare Island, 7765
  Norfolk, 7764
  Philadelphia, 7485
  Puget Sound, 7771
  San Francisco, 8159
[Recruiting]
  General, 9470
  Inspector of:
    Central Division, 9963, 56475
    Eastern Section, 9880
    Northeastern Division, 56368
    Southeastern Division, 56417
    Southern District, 9881
    Western Division, 9882, 9467
  Parties, traveling, 522
  Policy, 7045
  Posters, 545
  Rendezvous, 5198
  System, circular letters, 6974
Red Cross, American, 7487
Registry notices, 1097
Rejection reports, 1257
Relics, 1130
Relief, 3777
Relief movements, 6118
Religion, 5805
Remains, 2045
Requisitions, 3099
Rescues, 4388

Reserve Fire Corps, 6328
Reserve officers, 9354
Resurrection Bay, 6070
Returns, 1624
Revenue Cutter Service, 2206
Revenue cutters and Service, 3114
Revised Statutes & Statutes at Large, 5584
Rules of the road, 5158

Salutes, 685, 6188
Salvage operations, 40148
Santo Domingo, condition of affairs in, 5266
School ships, 3838
Scientific surveys, 6238
Scientific work, 2882
Scouts photography, 8775
Sea and shore duty, 5283
Seals, 3857
Seaman gunners, 597, 5557
Secret code lockers, 6270
Secret codes, 1023, 2783
Shipments, 3610, 57355
Shipping articles, 3239
Ships
  Agents on, 5838
  Coaling, 681
  Dutch, 30689
  Equipment of, 2127
  Hospital, 1810, (1915), 8151
  Libraries on, 2835
  School, 3838
  Supply (1914), 8158
  Training, 1493, 2375
  See also Vessels.
Signal books, 981
Signal numbers, 3293
Signaling, 1380
Small arms, 5195; firing regulations for, 4262
Social register, 4300
Socialists, 6182
Society Islands, 5303
Soldiers and sailors clubs, 3449
Spanish-American War, 2062; commanders of, 4290
Speaking trumpets, 6247

Sponsors for launchings, 7796
Staff officer nominations, S.& A, M &.S, C & R, and Y & D, 56989
State Department, 1328
Statistics, 523, 5539
Steam Engineering, Bureau of, 2838
Steaming trials, 6334
Stores, 647
Stragglers, 979
Structural materials, 5771
Submarine boats, 1817, 2725
Submarine chasers, 10973
Subsistence, 1021, 57369
Suggestions, offers of, 18312
Supplies and Accounts, Bureau of, 1815, 2546
Supply ships, 1914, 8158
Surgeons, assistant, 4826

Tableware, 4268
Tactical data, 6342
Target practice, 1506, 5688
Targets, 1644
Telegrams, 1868
Telegraph and cable companies, 612
Telephone service, 5510
Temperance, 1651
Textbooks, 6236
Tonnage certificates, 1088
Torpedo boats, 3545
Torpedo Boats in Reserve, Norfolk, 874
Torpedo destroyers, 1858
Torpedo men, 31237
Torpedoes, mines, and mining, 778, 6337
Trade schools, general, 14012
Training services, 5274
Training ships, 1493, 2375
Transfer, 7154; of hospital appropriations, 1027; of drafts [of men], 984; of men, 3281
Transport, 1914, 8163
Transportation, 588, 5141, 5399, 7340, 57362

Transportation (continued)
  Bids, 2559
  Civilians, 7352
  Reports, 3844
  Schedules, 3712
Transports, 3248
Traveling expenses, 721
Treasury, Department of, 2296
Trial courses, 5335
Trophies, 4437
Tugs, 1716
Turbine engines, 6327
Turkey, affairs in, 4067

Uniform regulations, 2390
Uniforms, 774, 5537, 57370
Uruguay, 3323

Vaccination, 6006
Venezuela, affairs in, 521, 6152
Vessels: for sale, 1667; foreign, 1536; in reserve, 6338; merchant, 40949; movements of, 3740; new, 2036; old, 2408; repair of, 5307. See also Ships.
Vicksburg National Park, 5919
Virgin Islands, 11126
Visitors, 2866
Visits of ceremony, 561, 5566
Volunteer Naval Reserve, 9877
Volunteers, 8575; in European War, 8957; war, 520
Vouchers, 3311

[War College]
  General, 57904, 1453
  Appropriations, 57904-05
  Complements, 57904-04
  Contracts and schedules, 57904-01
  Estimates, 57904-06
  Requisitions, 57904-02
  Schools, 57904-03
War diary, 14400
War Department, 837, 1411
War in China, 2361
War in Philippines, 3906
War machinery, 859

War risk insurance, 21417
War slate, 7779
Water barges, 3684, 4370
Weather warning, 969
Welfare organizations, 55400
Whereabouts, 2004, 57356
White House, 2879
Wireless telegraph operators, 3827
Wireless telegraphy, 1643
Wireless telephones, 5980
Wood and timber, 2997
Wrecks, 854
Wrecks and derelicts, 6162

[Yards]
   General, 6149
   Boston, 3452
   Charleston, 3642

[Yards] (continued)
   League Island, 2761
   Mare Island, 2743; complement, 3583
   New York, 2403
   Norfolk, 2824
   Organization, 6548
   Pensacola, 4348; complement, 1923
   Portsmouth, 4099
   Puget Sound, 2362
   Washington, 4294; complement, 2698
Yards and Docks, Bureau of, 5707
Yeomen, 5204

ZR1-1 [dirigible Shenandoah], 57421

www.ingramcontent.com/pod-product-compliance
Lightning Source LLC
Chambersburg PA
CBHW080557090426
42735CB00016B/3264